THE HAND
AND ITS MYSTERIES

First Published by
Philip Allan & CO in 1924

This facsimile edition has been carefully scanned
and reprinted in the traditional manner by
THE LOST LIBRARY
5 High Street,
Glastonbury UK BA6 9DP

The LOST LIBRARY is a publishing house based in
Glastonbury, UK, dedicated to the reproduction
of important rare esoteric and scholarly texts for
the discerning reader.

Cataloguing Information
The Hand and its Mysteries
Karma

ISBN 978 1 906621 22 3

Printed by Replika Press Pvt Ltd,
Haryana, India

**THE LOST
LIBRARY**

THE HAND
AND ITS MYSTERIES

AN OLD OCCULT SCIENCE
EXPLAINED & ILLUSTRATED

BY

KARMA

IN TWO BOOKS

I. CHEIROMANCY
II. ANCIENT PALMISTRY

LONDON
PHILIP ALLAN & CO.
QUALITY COURT
1924

*Uniform with this
volume.*

ASTROLOGY
OF THE ANCIENT
EGYPTIANS

BY

KARMA

—

A book for all who are
interested in the occult
sciences, and in particular
that branch of them which
deals with horoscopes and
the influence of the stars
upon nativity and life.

INTRODUCTION

THIS book is an epitome of the literature of the past ages dealing with Cheiromancy.

I have verified, and in some cases corrected, these ancient methods from practical experience on the subject : this enables me to give a comprehensive and reliable system.

This old occult science, having its foundation in the Divine light of Nature—which has always a character and expression of her own—will foreshadow the coming events of the Life, Fame, Power, and Fortune ; for the hand is the active servant of the mind, and " the mind is the hand of the soul."

TABLE OF CONTENTS

BOOK I

CHEIROMANCY

TABLE OF CONTENTS

BOOK II

ANCIENT PALMISTRY

TABLE OF CONTENTS

LIST OF ILLUSTRATIONS

BOOK I

BOOK II

xi

LIST OF ILLUSTRATIONS

IN THE TEXT

BOOK I

CHEIROMANCY

Nature is read too much by the illusive light of romance—rather than by the true character of her own language.

A

1

REFLECTIONS

CHEIROMANCY is an old occult science which helps one to understand the temperament and the character, teaching one how to read these hidden mysteries from the formation of the hands, with the lines and symbols to be seen in the palms. These ancient sciences—Astrology and Cheiromancy—lift up the thoughts from the material world and its artificial channels, to the abstract-concrete forms of knowledge ; refining and etherealizing the mind, helping those who study and love nature's language to penetrate the inner soul of her wonders, and learn practical wisdom.

So ancient is this language of the hands, that its discovery is lost in very remote antiquity ; it is almost as old as Astrology.

From very early times it was studied by eminent philosophers—Hermes, Plato, Homer, Aristotle, and the Ptolemies—those super-minds of medieval Egypt. These venerable sages, and divinely inspired ones, made an intense research of nature's language, seeking the foundation of truth in its hidden elements. The thoughts of these great minds have lived throughout the ages —through thousands of years.

They have left us the results of their investigations, their opinions and ideas upon this art of divination as indicated by the shape of the hands, with the scores and signs marked upon the palms. There is no doubt the ancients realized the value of this science of Cheiromancy in its relation to the character, and so the destiny, of man, regarding it as worthy of esteem and honour ; for in those far-off centuries Man's greatest study was Man.

There is an account of Aristotle when visiting Egypt finding a papyrus relating to Cheiromancy written in letters of gold, upon an altar dedicated to Hermes, which was transmitted to Alexander as a study worthy the attention of some highly cultivated intelligence.

Although so many of these rare and curious writings of the wise ones of early times have been unfortunately destroyed, still the pathway remains for those who search after, and love, the wisdom of the past ; seeing in its revelation a power to help man not only to understand him-

4

self but his fellow creatures ; rising upon the pinions of light to a higher intelligence and greater ideals.

To seek after and investigate knowledge which is out of reach or hidden has always intrigued the human mind ; and deeply implanted in the heart is the love of divination, bringing into union the conscious and sub-conscious minds— reason and imagination—which Hermes speaks of as Earth and Fire.

Herbert Spencer said : " There is produced a further habit of thought not otherwise produced, which is essential to right thinking in general by cultivation of the abstract-concrete sciences."

A particular training of one's thoughts is necessary before one can fully understand and grasp the exoteric and esoteric meaning of this science of Cheiromancy ; the mind must adopt an analytical and impersonal point of view. One of the writers on this subject has said : " A certain sense of relation is requisite to the student who would study the science, a sense which develops itself as the subject unfolds itself."

The great minds of the past who have made their fellow creatures their study have attached importance to the hands ; it is also the most ancient and universal form of divination ; for centuries ago this science was practised by the Brahmins of India, the ancient Greeks, and the Egyptians—generations that were essentially gifted with the powers of prevision and the faculty of prescience.

Aristotle says : " Because Man was the wisest of all animals he was given hands."

Amongst the modern investigators of this interesting cult the names of M. d'Arpentigny and Adrien Desbarrolles stand pre-eminent as the re-discoverers of this almost forgotten language. Having so strong a foundation in truth and nature it has survived the ages.

D'Arpentigny made a thorough investigation of the writings of the Ancients ; being much impressed and interested in the literature of the past on the science, he learnt much that was to be known ; desiring further to understand this subject he then began to put his knowledge into practice by comparing the hands of those with whom he came in contact. He found, after years of close study and investigation, that it was a system based on logic and reason. Cheiromancy is a *science* which explains the character, temperament, mental attributes, and the health, by the formation and condition of the hands : this science includes Palmistry, which makes known the whole destiny for good or evil.

REFLECTIONS

Cheiromancy being so open to fraud and deceit has from time to time been used by the unscrupulous and ignorant ; pretending to practise and understand it, but not having the necessary talents, they have brought this old-world science into disrepute and ignominy by their absurd deductions, making it considered of little worth ; but it has once more arisen from the dangers that have so often menaced and denounced it.

Cheiromancy is a *science* fixed and physical. Henry Drummond says : " A fully explained science is not only unknown, but non-existent."

The markings and signs on the hands have nothing to do with physical work ; for the labouring classes who carry out the manual work of the world have very few lines, and those are broad and coarse in the manner in which they are scored upon the palms. In relation to this the following paragraph from Quain's *Anatomy* is of interest :

> " These furrows are not merely the consequence of the frequent folding of the skin by the action of muscles, or the bending of joints, for they exist in the embryo."

After many years of study and thought on this old mystical science one comes to the opinion that these markings and symbols are principally made by the sub-conscious mind : it is the inner life and thoughts, the soul, that writes this indelible language on the hands ; and may not the *future* be known to the *soul* ? For these outer physical signs " half reveal and half conceal the soul within." The temperament and the character with its many attributes, capacities, talents and faults, are undoubtedly indicated.

This science of Cheiromancy is correlative, so do not judge by one sign alone : they are to be understood as running concurrently, not consecutively.

The direction of the character and tendencies of temperament can be seen in the hands of quite young children—the hand in type is definitely fixed by the age of fifteen. " Know Thyself " : how seldom it is that one finds this wise maxim of the ancient Greeks put into practice, and least of all by parents in relation to their children ! Cheiromancy warns one of the sunken rocks that are deeply hidden in the temperament, rocks upon which a career may strike and on which are wrecked so many lives.

Nature has stamped her potent truths on everything around us, and all knowledge has originated from natural phenomena.

The mind gains rest and renewed strength by

the study of elementary principles, and the observation of common things teaches one wisdom.

Cheiromancy illustrates two wise and beautiful maxims : " Know Thyself," and " Understand Others." For to judge anyone without prejudice or malice is to see their point of view through *their* temperament and not *one's own*, which is only personal and relative to oneself. So many are prepossessed with unexamined opinions. The different shaped hands have always a tendency to proceed through life true to their type—for one cannot expect the person with the big palmed hand to have the same ideas and natural instincts as the man with a small palm and long tapering fingers, or expect a soft hand to have naturally the energy of the hard type.

SECTION 1

HANDS AND THEIR SIGNIFICATIONS

1

HANDS AND THEIR SIGNIFICATIONS

THE VARIOUS TYPES.

THE old cheiromantists classified the hands into seven types. They are :

The Elementary

The large-palmed hand, with thick inflexible fingers.

The Spatulate

The necessary or useful hand : the active workers.

The Square

The hand of order, method and arrangement.

The Conical

The artistic : it is more the hand of thought and ideas.

The Philosophic

The knotted hand : it questions, argues and examines.

THE HAND

The Psychic

This is the thin, very pointed hand : it is ethereal and idealist.

The Mixed Hand

This is undecided in outline, belonging to two different types and sometimes three.

These seven types of hands are as varied in shape and form as the leaves of a tree. On this subject Desbarrolles says :

" Hands may resemble one another, but nature never repeats herself, and in objects apparently the most similar she places, sometimes by an imperceptible touch, a complete diversity of instincts."

And each type obeys its own occult law; but the development of the character, which is shown by the Head Line, can modify the temperament ; but not beyond a certain point, for the fundamental tendencies in the nature are persistent. Education and culture will develop the reflective powers of reason, and so oppose and keep in check these spontaneous elements of our animal instincts.

Man has two great forces which he obeys :

Temperament : this comprises the natural instincts—desires and inclinations—the exoteric or generalities ; and

HANDS AND THEIR SIGNIFICATIONS

Character : which is the mind : the conscious, the objective, that reasons and calculates ; and the sub-conscious, the subjective, that *knows*— which is the esoteric, or particularities.

Confucius said :

" To love one's fellow creatures is a virtue, to know them is a science, and to despise them is the ruin of virtue."

" Study yourself, perfect yourself, be simple in heart, and love your neighbour as yourself."

SECTION 2

THE CHARACTERISTICS OF THE ELEMENTARY HAND

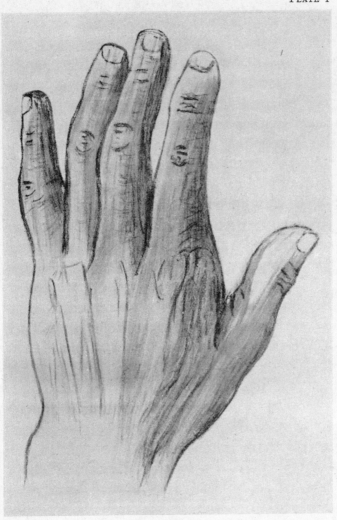

PLATE I

THE ELEMENTARY HAND

2

THE CHARACTERISTICS OF THE
ELEMENTARY HAND

THIS is a big, heavy, clumsy type of hand—
the fingers unpliant and shapeless—the palms
excessively big, hard and thick ; this being the
chief characteristic—with the whole hand inflexible.

Intended by nature to undertake manual
labour and coarse work—which may be carried
out purely by instinct, proceeding mechanically
and by habit.

This elementary hand indicates a dull imagination, and feelings heavy, inactive and indifferent, having no great desire either to read
or write, being slow of understanding and
difficult to inspire with any kind of enthusiasm.
This type of hand is found more among the far
northern countries—such as the Laplanders, who
escape the evils of that climate by their sheer
inertness—and in its pure type among natives

of Tartar or Sclavonic origin—indicating, when roused, brutal, cruel and ferocious natures. In more civilised countries we do not see this pure type, but the quasi-elementary, and this is modified and transformed by the times and its environment.

To hands of this class we owe the culture of those gardens where the vegetables and aromatic herbs are kept flourishing and smiling. This type is more often seen among the rustic dwellers of farms and villages than those of cities, Nature having great uses for these elementary hands ; for they carry out all the coarse employments, having little imagination or refinement. But they are necessary and are the pioneers of civilisation. Their spirituality is at the stage of superstition ; they feel and fear more the powers of the intangible forces in nature than the love of the Divine Spirit.

Not having those resources of the mind and soul that give moral strength to the other types, they more readily succumb to temptation, pain and disappointments ; but they have much bodily prowess, though little initiative ; their minds work in a groove ; they understand only their bodily instincts and material requirements ; they are strangers to all progress, labour appearing more important than knowledge or skill ;

they have no reasons for their ideas and actions, but they have obstinate convictions.

The only refining element accessible to these dull and inert natures is music ; for they do not realise the wonders of science, nor are they conscious of the imaginative realms of the poetic and romantic.

As is the hand, so is the mind.

PLATE II

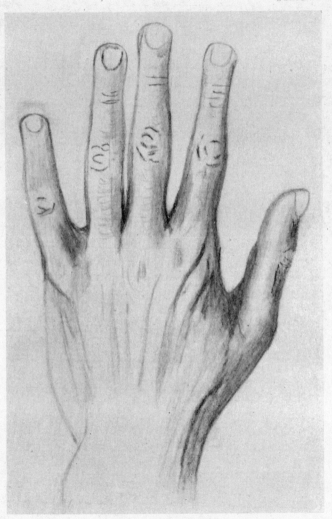

THE SPATULATE HAND

SECTION 3

THE CHARACTERISTICS OF THE
SPATULATE HAND

3

THE CHARACTERISTICS OF THE
SPATULATE HAND

THIS large spatulate hand with a big thumb is more numerous in northern latitudes, where action and movement are necessary to man for his protection and material needs. It is called spatulate because the nail phalanges of the fingers present the appearance of a spatula, an instrument that a dispensing chemist uses in making up his prescriptions.

This is the active industrious type, having an instinctive intelligence, being resourceful when combating physical obstacles ; delighting in an active and energetic life, being devoted to sport and games ; loving to subjugate the material world by their physical strength and natural intelligence ; having much self-confidence and resolution.

All the famous navigators, hunters, great explorers and athletes, throughout the ages, are represented as having had this type of hand.

THE HAND

It is found more often in England, Scotland, America, Germany, and in northern and mountainous countries. Appreciating utility before beauty, putting comfort before luxury, admiring energy, activity and strength, these spatulate hands indicate more judgment than imagination.

Constancy in love is denoted ; for being not easily swayed by the charms of beauty or romance, they are influenced more by custom or duty, and so are reliable in affection.

D'Arpentigny says :

> " The old fighting nobility devoted to war, the chase, and the tournament had this type of hand ; and this energy and activity was noted as one of the chief characteristics of the ancient Romans—seeming to care for nothing but war and the pleasures of the senses."

When this spatulate hand is supple, with smooth slim fingers and a smaller thumb, it denotes great appreciation of comfort and abundance, preferring " la mode " and the elegant to the exquisite and harmonious. Should these fingers be longer than the palm, it denotes wit —versatility and intuition. The histrionic arts have a fascination for this type of hand : they prefer artistic work that has movement and action.

THE SPATULATE HAND

Women with this type of hand are often attracted to the medical or scientific professions : they make good nurses and travellers, having much physical energy and endurance.

When these spatulate fingers are found shorter than the palm, it denotes sensuality in love, liking the material side of life and its pleasures, devoted to field sports, often daring and courageous. Being endowed with much common sense, there is always a reason for their activity.

Instrumentalists in music as a rule have spatulate hands, with small thumbs.

D'Arpentigny says that the celebrated pianist Liszt had a very large hand of this type, denoting fineness of work and a talent for detail and finish ; the fingers being prominently jointed denoted precision ; the wide spatulate tips announced strength in execution. In his hands he had the power of a whole orchestra, entrancing his audiences with his ardour, passion, and impetuosity, but never losing his self-possession. It is also said of another famous master in the musical world—the great and immortal Paganini—that he had this type of hand, very large and firm, but with the exterior phalanges more pointed.

These spatulate hands love movement, activity and industry, power and material advantages. When the joints are developed, having the talents of practical and mechanical sciences almost in perfection.

These are the hands that design the architecture of a utilitarian order, having constructive abilities and engineering talents, building bridges, streets and factories, and the organisation and combination of great industries.

The smooth spatulate hand, hard and strong, is always an athlete, fond of expeditions and explorations.

One of the old writers on this subject says : " Hercules is the god of the spatulate type."

This is the hand that loves freedom and unconventionality.

SECTION 4

THE CHARACTERISTICS OF THE SQUARE HAND

PLATE III

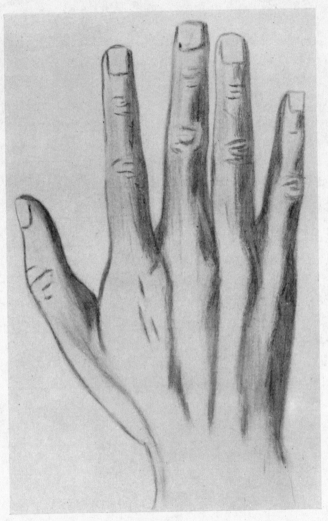

THE SQUARE HAND

4

THE CHARACTERISTICS OF THE SQUARE HAND

THIS hand is large rather than small, with the outer phalanges of the fingers square, that is the two sides extend parallel to the tips, and the fingers more often have slightly developed joints.

The palm is of medium size, firm, with a rather long, well-developed thumb. It is one of the useful hands, being orderly, methodical, practical, with continuity and precision.

With a large thumb they have very little imagination, only believing in the tangible, quick to deny anything that they do not understand or experience ; knowing little of the world of ideas, having thoughts which they may extend, but by which they never rise ; attaching more importance to common-sense than to genius, to the real than the ideal ; conforming to the conventionalities, being a little suspicious of anything that is out of the ordinary or extreme, living by rule and custom.

These are two useful types : the spatulate hand—admiring all that is physically powerful, graceful, and that which pleases by being " the glass of fashion : " and the square hand—all that is orderly and according to custom and tradition, with great respect for power and position.

Some of the great masters in the world of music, principally the composers, had these square hands, giving them the talent for time and measure with musical rhythm.

These square-handed people are ruled by method and organisation ; they are often narrow-minded and despotic, having more brains than heart.

This square type has great commercial talents, and endowed with instincts for political and social life. They cultivate the practical with moderate, but positive, ideas, with a great sense of duty, either in the world or in the home life, loving order, method and custom ; but with little sense of romance or flights of imagination.

The forms and customs of the Chinese illus-trate the characteristics of the square-handed type—for it is found in the majority in that country—for the height of their social virtues is politeness and tact, with strict attention to certain forms and customs.

Architecture, under the sway of this square type of hand, is materially useful, but with a wearisome symmetry, giving one an impression of arithmetic rather than poetry.

To this type of hand " The stars in their courses do not sing," for the planets have no further meaning to them beyond their physical attributes which can be measured, weighed, and their natural conditions understood ; this square type is endowed with the great talents of comparison and proportion, but they never get beyond physical realities, earth being their domain ; they are conscious of nothing beyond the material life of man.

This is the type that has the mind of reason and calculation strongly developed ; the other half of the mind, the sub-conscious, is usually dormant.

SECTION 5

THE CHARACTERISTICS OF THE
CONICAL HAND

PLATE IV

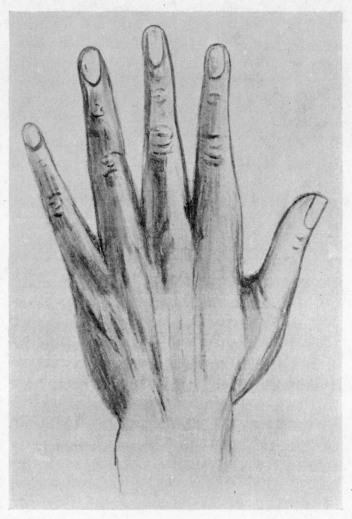

THE CONICAL HAND

THE CHARACTERISTICS OF THE CONICAL HAND

THIS is the artistic hand, having three very decided tendencies, all three forms obeying inspiration. In appearance the fingers are inclined to be thick and full at the roots, getting gradually thinner up to the tips, which are pointed, like a drawn-out cone. The thumb, as a rule, is small and pliant, with a palm fairly well developed.

If broad, thick and short, with a large thumb, it gives a desire for greatness, glory and fortune, proceeding by stratagem and artifice.

When supple and moderately developed, with a small thumb, it indicates the love of the beautiful in form and colour, drawn instinctively to the imaginative and picturesque, without reflection or reason, only observing material order, as it conforms to an aid to beauty. Large and thick, this type of hand tends to the material side of life, and the sensual side of pleasures. These three artistic types are temperamental, passing from moods of deep despair to stages of excitement and enthusiasm, having more impetuosity and ardour than reliance and power, impulse being their guide and rarely duty.

They are difficult for the other types to understand or live with, as they have so little sense of order, prudence or usefulness ; often being eccentric in manner and dress, as they view everything as they imagine it to be; proceeding through life by impulse, passion, and fancy.

A large palmed hand with conical fingers and a small turned back thumb, with a short will phalanx, indicates a fickle temperament, possessing more sentiment than heart, proceeding through life by the promptings of pleasure, idle, careless and capricious.

With a large, strong thumb, this type of hand will intrigue and scheme for riches and power ; with thick fingers, developing a love of vulgar display of money.

These artistic hands with flexible fingers and filbert nails, with a supple and moderately developed palm, and a small pliant thumb, obey the passion, inspiration, and artistic instincts of their being.

The conical hand with the turned back thumb

belongs more to the southern races, with their charm and grace—the Celts, Latins, Egyptians and Orientals.

These artistic hands originate and are full of ideas. D'Arpentigny said : " The ancient monuments and temples of Memphis, Thebes, Babylon, and Assyria owe their glorious beauty to these inspired hands."

They have great appreciation and understanding of exquisite colours, proportion, and form, in relation to beauty and art. These true artistic instincts cannot be taught, they must be inborn.

The souls of these artistic hands have an adoration for music, this type being so often seen among opera singers and vocalists, denoting a love of melody in music ; preferring the beautiful and harmonious to the fashion of the moment, adornment and luxury to ease or comfort. Mechanical or domestic work never attracts them, and if necessary it would be undertaken against the temperament.

The famous soldiers throughout the ages who possessed this conical type of hand have certainly been picturesque figures, but it is a matter of history that they preferred glory and fame to military success. D'Arpentigny describes Napoleon's hand as being the hard conical type—

broad, short, rather thick, with pointed fingers and a large thumb ; showing the desire for greatness and glory.

This type of hand can be very enthusiastic, with much intuition, inspiration, and faith, with a passionate belief in their " Star."

These artistic hands always belong to romantic natures : they love everything that is brilliant and splendid, even in their ruin and poverty.

SECTION 6

THE CHARACTERISTICS OF THE
PHILOSOPHIC HAND

PLATE V

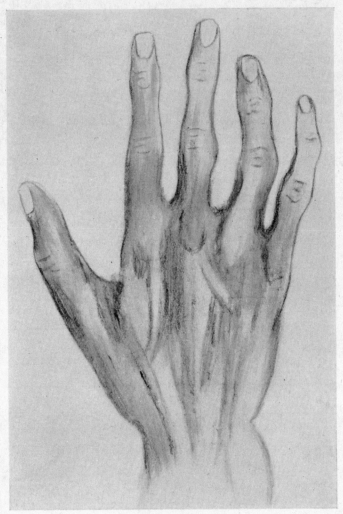

THE PHILOSOPHIC HAND

THE CHARACTERISTICS OF THE
PHILOSOPHIC HAND

THIS is the knotty type, with the palm rather large and well developed ; the joints well marked in the fingers, the tips being a combination of half square and half conical ; generally with a large thumb—the two phalanges of will and reason being of equal length.

This hand is divided into two classes : the idealists and the sensualists. The finger-tips very pointed with these developed joints will make them idealists ; with often a subtle and abstract mind—very difficult for others to understand, as they are inclined to isolate themselves in thought and ideas, without passion or love, but always with a desire for reason and truth. It is the essence of things and not their form or beauty that they try to understand.

These philosophic hands have calculation, method and deduction ; feeling that reason and faith are a more reliable guide than intuition or love. They proceed by analysis, where the smooth fingers aim at synthesis.

The knotty hand with spatulate finger-tips is a type that is drawn to that which is useful in the material world. If with square tips, to practical ideas, with combination and calculation, giving them great talent for science, research, exploring and mathematics, with method and precision. These hands have always a keen sense of time and order, leaning towards practical ideas and realities—when in extreme, exacting about punctuality and tidiness.

The knotty hands with conical or pointed finger-tips tend to speculative ideas and often strange beliefs.

The philosophic hands with large thumbs are guided by their head—they analyse ; with small thumbs they are led by their heart—and inclined to synthesis. The chief defect of these philosophic hands is that they often seem fanatical over any belief that attracts them and which has very little foundation to rest upon.

They are conscious of the internal world, and have an unquenchable love for deep metaphysics and philosophical sciences ; they are inspired by the teachings of Socrates, who said that whatever injures one injures humanity in all that is holiest and truest.

SECTION 7

THE CHARACTERISTICS OF THE PSYCHIC HAND

PLATE VI

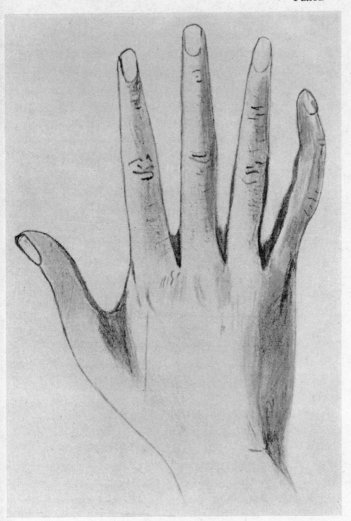

THE PSYCHIC HAND

7

THE CHARACTERISTICS OF THE PSYCHIC HAND

IN appearance it is small and fine—a medium palm, and smooth fingers, the nail phalanges long and pointed, the thumb small and slim. The psychic hand is not, as many writers of romances state, exclusively the hand of the noble and old families ; it is rare, and not a universal type, but it exists in all classes, and it is very much misunderstood and disdained by the ignorant, or those with the elementary hands, for this psychic hand has no aptitude for manual labour.

This type of hand is found more often in India than any other country, where they assert that the greatest sin is the desiring of material things rather than the love of the spiritual.

The square and spatulate hands have very little sympathy with the " psychic " characteristics, for they find neither method, order, activity, nor precision in mundane affairs of their own natures. For these " psychic hands " dwell in the spheres of spirit, living in their belief of intangible realities and the realms of the soul.

D'Arpentigny describes them as composed of " flame and light," while the other types are " flesh and blood." He says " a great gulf divides them, and two different languages are not too many for two natures so in extreme."

Hands of this type ruled India up to the thirteenth century, when they lost this temporal power, through having so little talent for the arts and skill in war, navigation and locomotion.

These psychic hands are more often found in southern, dreamy Asia than in the restless, laborious cities of Europe or America, with their trades, arts and sciences ; and so the hands that are necessary for this labour are drawn to them —and that is not the psychic hand, for it has little understanding of the needs of the material life : their genius dwells in high spheres—whence have arisen all the great religions.

Although this psychic hand belongs to mystics and spiritualistic minds, it is not free from temptations ; for the world of spirit is as perilous, and has its imperfections, as the world of man.

THE PSYCHIC HAND

D'Arpentigny refers to this hand as a noble type—he says :

> " Taken as a whole, these hands love great struggles and disdain little ones—represented by Plato—when Greek decadence held sway ; finding their archetype in the Christ when Roman sensualism was at its height."

Being a channel for the Divine Mind, their intervention has never failed when the other types with their material outlook have brought the affairs of nations to a state of chaos and confusion, when only a Divine agency can save the race of man, with his intelligence and dignity, from perishing ; for they give a calm mind and a resolute heart, with a faith in God, liberty, love of country, and the universal brotherhood of Man.

The thoughts indicated by the psychic hand are reflected in the works of Milton, Schiller, Lamartine, Goethe, Swedenborg, Chateaubriand, and those great world teachers Hermes, Orpheus, Plato, the Buddha, and the Christ. The subconscious mind, with a spiritual imagination, is highly developed in the psychic hand.

These types of hands, from the elementary to the psychic, are the different facets in the great jewel of humanity—all being of the one race of Man.

SECTION 8

THE CHARACTERISTICS OF THE MIXED HAND

PLATE VII

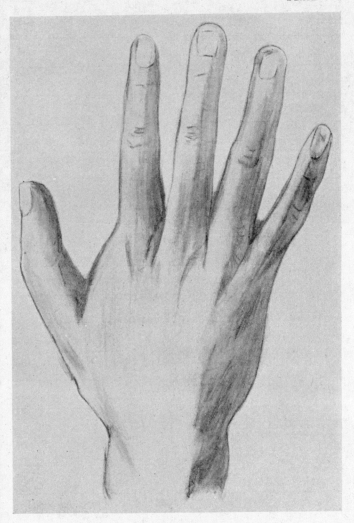

THE MIXED HAND

8

THE CHARACTERISTICS OF THE MIXED
HAND

IN appearance it might belong to two different types : for instance, a conical elementary hand might be taken for an artistic hand ; if spatulate the formation is so little accentuated that it might be taken for a square ; or a slightly philosophic hand for a spatulate.

These types of hands are rather inclined to be Jack-of-all-trades and master-of-none ; for excelling in no particular direction they never seem quite to know what career they want ; whereas a decided type has its promptings too strong to be disobeyed.

The great geniuses of the past that have divined on certain lines had hands of a decided and pronounced type, being powerful in one direction but not versatile—for it is the mixed hand that is adaptable and versatile—but they do not originate nor are they powerful in one direction of thought or work. But the mixed type of hand—socially and as companions—can be more generally amusing and entertaining.

D'Arpentigny says :

" It is to mixed hands that the intelligence of mixed works of intermediary ideas belong —it is relative to the realities of science, industry, and the beauties of art.—Just as there are absolute truths and absolute beauties, there are also relative ones."

It is this mixed hand that is relative ; it is found in the majority in America and Europe. If it is the mixed spatulate and square types, with a hard thick palm, slightly leaning towards the elementary, with a big thumb—it denotes talent for industry and commerce, a practising of the arts and sciences, eloquence, and even religion, but only to derive material benefits from them.

Another mixed hand that materialises everything is the elementary artistic type. It is the " smug " hand ; its one aim is money and power ; it can even pretend to virtue if there is material advantage to be gained by it. It has no love of perfection in art or science—for it can always substitute the imitation if there is money to be gained by it ; and glory without any material advantages would be ridiculous to it.

THE MIXED HAND

Euripides must have possessed this mixed type of hand, for he said : " A king in a state of poverty is nothing."

Wealth is what is most revered by men with this mixed type of hand—worshipping their god in the shape of the " almighty dollar." These hands are found in a great majority amongst the Jews, who are distinguished for their capacity for commerce and finance.

A mixed hand with a hard palm, a big thumb and conical finger-tips will be attracted to the professions of the broker, the merchant, the agent, the stock-jobber, the publican and the banker, in fact all the pursuits where quickness of mind and sharpness of wits are of more account than the gifts of art or music, great knowledge of science, or the genius and skill of mind and hands. These mixed hands measure happiness by the greatness of their belongings.

The psychico-artistic type of hand denotes the passion of their souls for the spirit of the Divine in the woods, when the verdant greens of spring are clothing the long sleeping trees in their pristine beauty of nature, and the smiling hyacinths are bending their gentle heads, listening to the winds of the south that whisper " the winter is past, we herald the spring "—at the feet of the golden flames of the sun and in the meadowsweet grass of early June; when they lie in dreams of far-off worlds of light on the flowery heath or in the starlight of a summer's night; living in worlds of fairy legends and the poetry of old; preferring meditation and repose to wealth and soul-stifling luxury; for this type of hand knows nothing of the sordid side of avarice and intriguing ambitions. Along a blest and radiant path they follow the soul of the Muse, with its perfumed air of mystical incense and flowers, wearing the diadem of faith, with happiness and a glory that illumines the way. The heart is seeking for and finding—Rest and Peace.

SECTION 9

THE SIGNS ATTACHED TO THE HANDS

9

THE SIGNS ATTACHED TO THE HANDS

(I)

FROM observation and deduction of the various types one finds the indications of the physical desires on the palm of the hand, and the intellectual aptitudes in the fingers—with the thumb as the index.

Intellectual power without physical force would only give " instincts without capacity "— a phase of character well known ; also physical force without the guiding power of reason would give proof of great stupidity of character.

Hands that have the appearance of being hard and stiff, and very set in one form, having difficulty in extending to their utmost limit, indicate an obstinate, stubborn nature and a mind without elasticity—the hand being the active agent of the thoughts, and " the thoughts being the hands of the soul."

THE HAND

Hands flexible and supple, with the fingers extending and apart, denote versatility, moderation, and independence of thought and action ; with a turned back thumb this type of hand signifies talent for the histrionic arts, and social adaptability.

Hard hands—one is endowed with much energy and activity; very hard—restlessness —the body being more active than the mind.

Soft hands indicate indolence, a love of luxury, with more mental than physical activity.

(2) The Palm of the Hand

A well-developed palm gives force to the character ; when broad it indicates a love of sport and country life.

A narrow and thin hand if very slim and small is lacking in physical power, and indicates a feeble nature ; if the palm is hollow, there is a want of vitality, a weak constitution. It is difficult for this type of hand to fight adverse circumstances.

The palm should be in proper proportion to the size of the fingers, of a medium thickness, neither too hard or too supple ; then the intellect will keep pace with the senses, and one will have a normal temperament and character.

The palm dominating the fingers by excessive

development indicates self-love, and self-interest with sensuality will be prominent in the nature.

When utterly out of proportion, and the thumb and fingers very thick and hard, it indicates one who is without imagination or ideas, with the physical instincts and desires very dominant. The indication given by the thumb and fingers will modify or confirm the signs on the palm, the thumb being the most important of all the fingers.

(3) THE THUMB

A long and well-shaped thumb shows one's descent from intellectual ancestors.

The thumb signalises the man as the hand does the animal; but it is only the race of man that has thumbs. Newton said : " In default of any other proof, the thumb would convince me of the existence of God."

In Cheiromancy the thumb is the chief signature of the moral force; for from it we judge the strength and endurance of the will, the reasoning faculties, and the power of the affections and sympathies.

A thumb that is over long, inclined to be heavy, makes one aggressive; if the nail phalanx is long, broad and thick, with a coarse hand— the tyrant.

The nail phalanx shows the strength of will, power of decision, and initiative.

The second phalanx gives the reasoning faculties—logic and judgment.

If the nail phalanx is broad and long, it indicates a strong will ; with the second in proportion, reason and good judgment ; and with the root of the thumb fairly large, love and sympathy ; also a strong constitution, denoting a well-balanced nature.

A long or broad " will " phalanx, even on a soft hand that indicates a naturally indolent temperament, shows that its possessor will work when necessary more than a naturally active nature with a short thumb, through a sense of duty, but with more mental energy than physical. A thumb which is small, meagre, and poorly formed, indicates a wavering character with an irresolute mind ; it shows little reasoning power, and is more often led by natural tendencies ; but at the same time it is tolerant, amiable, and adaptable to the different temperaments with whom it comes into contact.

A stiff-jointed thumb, which is characteristic of all northern races and is found principally among the Anglo-Saxon, North American, Germanic, and Dutch nationalities, denotes a stronger but less adaptable or pliable will than the thumb that turns back in either one phalanx or sometimes both. These flexible thumbs may not imply such strong characters as the stiff-jointed thumbs, but indicate adaptability with charm and grace. This type of thumb is more often found among the Celtic, Latin, and Southern races.

If in either type of thumb the reason phalanx —the second—is longer than the " will," that is the first or nail, phalanx—then it indicates making many plans, but not carrying them into action.

If this second phalanx of the thumb is waisted in shape, it will give refinement of thought and fastidiousness in dress and one's environment.

With the nail phalanx long and the reason phalanx short, one will act instinctively, without any great reason for what one does ; it denotes great convictions without judgment ; often wilful and, if broad, obstinate.

Those with large thumbs are governed by their head, being exclusive and reflective, preferring ideas to sentiment. With small thumbs they are governed by their hearts ; and if the mount at the base of the thumb where it joins the palm is full and firm, one will decide and judge by feelings and emotions, preferring sentiment to reason, often acting on impulse.

The large thumb gives naturally a stronger will ; its subjects have greater power to overcome the tendencies of temperament than those with small thumbs.

A very long thumb with the will and reason phalanges dominating, and a flat mount of Venus, would indicate a cold, unsympathetic nature, with a great desire to rule, but showing little mercy or understanding of human nature, especially if the thumb is stiff-jointed, on a long thin hand, with a narrow square palm ; these are the austere, unbending, cold natures, and most exacting over every detail.

A heavy-looking thumb shows selfishness. Turned in to the fingers it will give timidity. Turned back from the fingers and set low on the hand it will indicate a talented, adaptable, generous nature. If very much turned back—extravagance.

A pointed thumb announces frivolity and carelessness.

The nail phalanx thick and broad will make one obstinate.

A big, heavy thumb with the tip clubbed is always a fighter's thumb—the first impulse when put out of temper is to strike or throw something at the person who causes the annoyance. A heavy nail phalanx denotes a passionate temper.

A stiff-jointed thumb is one not bending back at either joint.

A flexible or supple thumb turns back in one and sometimes both joints.

A " waisted " thumb is one having the appearance of being cut away at either side, curving in from the nail phalanx to the second joint, that joins the root to the thumb.

(4) Hard and Soft Hands

Hands should be firm without being hard, and supple without being flabby. If they harden very gradually—a very firm hand more often becomes extremely hard—these temperaments seldom have tenderness in their love ; whilst soft hands have more tenderness than love.

Those with hard hands are restless, desiring action and movement.

The soft hand appreciates the charms of luxury and comfort—and not too much exertion.

Large hands, when firm, are a sign of physical strength ; with a medium development of the palms—one preferring finish to what is splendid, and the exquisite to the grand. The finest work is done by these—often enormous—hands.

The standard of beauty as applied to the hands by the Greeks was large, with strong, smooth, square-tipped fingers, a medium-sized palm, and a long slim thumb, as may be seen in their beautiful statues.

Small hands are attracted and affect not only the magnificent and enormous, but they admire and desire the huge, the gigantic ; they love everything on a great scale—their very details are big and immense, especially if they are very small pointed hands—indicating the laws of contrast.   One of the old writers on this subject says :

" Those colossal and magnificent Temples of the East and the Pyramids of Egypt were designed and built by these exquisite little hands."

The hands of the Oriental races are the most delicate in appearance in the world.

The bas-reliefs with which these structures are ornamented have representations of these small, delicate-looking hands—the hands that carried out these vast works.

The small hand indicates breadth of treatment.   The large hand denotes love of *minutiæ* and finish.

SECTION 10

THE JUDGMENT OF THE FINGERS

10

THE JUDGMENT OF THE FINGERS

(1)

FINGERS are either long or short, smooth or knotty. Those with long, smooth fingers do not analyse but proceed by intuition, for they do not reason or criticise. A hand showing natural talent will work by inspiration, fantasy, and imagination ; they incline to worry over details, not only concerning themselves but others, often about matters that are not important ; loving trifles and " finish."

When these long fingers are knotted it indicates a reflective mind, making for punctuality and tidiness, loving harmony and arrangement, preferring the scientific point of view, criticising and analysing the thoughts and ideas.

If the knot is on the nail phalanx it denotes mental order, well-regulated ideas.

If the joint which connects the second phalanx

with the lower one is prominent, it will indicate a gift for material order and method.

When the fingers are set into the hand, with prominent joints, and that part of the palm broad, it gives order in the domestic or home life, with talent for management and arrangement—a well-ordered house.

These long, knotted fingers indicate intellectual taste ; the long, smooth fingers denote instinctive grace.

When these long fingers are pointed it announces idealism ; if too pointed they are not practical, without method.

Square fingers denote order, method, and practical ideas. When the fingers are spatulate —activity and physical energy.

With short fingers, they do not care to enter into details, especially if they are the smooth fingers, judging everything *en masse*, making one impulsive and quick in movement, forming opinions hastily ; when pointed they indicate a romantic and idealistic nature.

If these short fingers are knotted, their possessors can be critical and fault-finding.

Pointed and knotted fingers tend towards the philosophical sciences—loving freedom and moderation in all things.

If with square tips and knotted, there is a

love . of science, order, and utility. When knotted and spatulate, the tendency is towards that which is materially useful.

It is an advantage for the square and spatulate fingers to be knotty, as they both belong to the useful hands, and these knotty joints give them calculation and combination—they are the practical temperaments. But to pointed or conical fingers it is a great drawback, as they proceed in thought by intuition, imagination, and inspiration—being the artistic temperaments.

When all the fingers are different in character as to their nail phalanges and are set clumsily on the hand, it indicates a want of intellectual development and strength of mind.

The tips of the fingers are considered the eyes of the hand, and when they have little pointed cushions they give great intuition by touch.

Long fingers are slow in coming to a decision or carrying out their plans ; they are deliberate in speech, inclined to worry and be fastidious about details, being more inquisitive than the short fingers, who are careless about finish and *minutiæ*, taking up many interests and, if a conical hand, tiring quickly, and leaving most things unfinished; lacking patience, and being too hasty about results ; restless and impulsive.

Fingers should be the same length as the palm—neither set or stiff, nor too flexible or limp; for the thoughts are represented by the fingers.

Fingers should be set upon an even line across the palm; any finger out of line—by being set too high or low on the hand—will not be normal in its characteristics—this telling against the character.

(2) THE FIRST FINGER—JUPITER

If well developed and straight on a pointed hand it denotes intuition, wisdom and justice. When square it indicates reasoning power and logic. Spatulate, it denotes energy and appreciation of material comfort. If this finger is very long, and pointing outwards, it gives to the temperament love of domineering and self-assertion, great personal pride. When short it inclines to a dislike of responsibilities, and if crooked and leaning towards the second finger it indicates deceit and hypocrisy.

(3) THE SECOND FINGER—SATURN

It is not an advantage to have this finger much longer than the others, as it then makes the nature too cautious, apprehensive and hopeless. When straight, not too heavy in appearance, and a little longer than the other fingers, it will then indicate prudence, discrimination, reflection, and faithfulness in love, a liking for agriculture and, with a clever Head-Line, mechanical genius.

These characteristics in the woman's hand show that she will prefer the home life, being domesticated, to a career in the world; and with the Mount of Venus well developed her greatest love will be for her children, and she will feel her nature unfulfilled if she does not become a mother.

(4) THE THIRD FINGER—APOLLO, OR THE SUN

The third finger—called Apollo, or the Sun—is next in importance to the thumb, giving talent and initiative, more than any of the other fingers. This is the finger that indicates the success of the life or career, portending riches and celebrity. It should be straight and rather long, not leaning towards either the second or fourth fingers; it will then bestow an optimistic and happy outlook on life, making the nature like a ray of sunshine, tolerant in opinion, with charm and grace of manner; giving enterprise, daring to take a risk to gain or lose the desire. It is not good for this finger to be too long as it then makes the gambler, not only with money, but life itself, with a love of continual change and excitement.

When on a conical or pointed hand it announces great love of art, music, and literature, refinement and good taste ; if the fingers are very pointed, with this third one long, it denotes an inclination to idealism and fantasy. On a square hand it indicates love of wealth.

With the spatulate hand it gives the spirit of adventure. When with knotty fingers, it makes the temperament inventive and mathematical.

With this finger long and the mount of Venus prominent one inclines to ardour and romance in love, but it does not denote constancy—unless the " will " phalanx of the thumb is long or broad. When this finger of Apollo leans towards the finger of Mercury—that is the little finger—it gives talent for speaking or writing ; it also inclines the nature to be restless, liking change and variety.

Clinging to the second—the Saturn finger— it will give morbid moods and depression, often making the temperament egoistical and selfish.

(5) THE FOURTH FINGER—MERCURY

For a successful career it is not a help to have this finger set low on the hand, for then it denotes that one is without the power to give expression to the thoughts or ideas, or the capacity for making use of one's talents, people, and opportunities. When straight, rather long, and set in an even line with the other fingers, with a pointed nail phalanx, it will give the spirit of intuition, quick perception, wit and eloquence ; with a square nail phalanx, science and administration. When spatulate, a talent for industrial or mechanical arts ; vivacity and movement. If crooked and over long, clinging to the third finger, it announces an inclination to sharp practice in business or affairs—one who will always take the advantage. In married life it is better for the woman not to have this finger long, for then she will be submissive, not desiring the last word in discussion or arguments. One of the old writers on this subject says :

" It brings happiness to a wife to have this finger short—she will then be naturally unselfish."

When fingers are thick at the base, pointed and shorter than the palm, it signifies love of luxury and self-indulgence—but with refinement and good taste.

Fingers very close together, with a hand that never quite opens out and the thumb turned in, show avarice and secretiveness.

Fingers with a perceptible space in between

them—that is when held up to the light—denote generosity and an inclination to be a spendthrift. This type of hand can never save. D'Arpentigny says :

> " Very long thin fingers with flattened tips are usually those of card-sharpers, pickpockets, deceivers, and liars."

Fingers long, supple, and turning back denote sagacity, curiosity, fascination, and charm of manner.

Cheiromancy has divided the fingers into the three worlds of Soul, Mind, and Body :

If the nail phalanges are long they indicate spirituality ; with the second phalanges longer than the other two—a forceful, clever mind. And those who are slaves to the appetites of the body, loving material pleasures, will have the lowest phalanges longest, and very full.

Extremely thick and short fingers indicate greed and cruelty.

———————

By knotty fingers is meant enlargement of the finger joints.

Smooth fingers : When the joints are scarcely apparent, on some hands almost imperceptible.

The phalanges are the three segments of the fingers and thumb.

(6) THE NAILS OF THE HAND

The nails are great indicators of the health. When long, narrow, and very thin, they show a delicate constitution ; also high or curved, a tendency to consumption—that is when seen on a soft, limp, damp hand.

Hard, brittle, fluted nails, with a thick red hand, indicate gout and rheumatism in the system.

Nails very flat and deeply dented, sometimes broken in the centre, denote toxic poisoning in the system, ill-health, and nervous disorders.

" Filbert-shaped " nails show a tendency to colds and relaxed throat ; when narrow, a weakness of the back, and kidney trouble, especially if the nails have patches of white and red.

Nails showing very big " moons " warn one of over action of the heart.

Nails without " moons," or very little showing, would indicate slow action of the heart.

The hand showing ill-health, with short broad nails that are very thin, often denotes a weak stomach and trouble with the intestines ; if very white in colour, a bad circulation.

Blood illnesses of all kinds—cancer, typhoid, consumption, or poison through bad food or foul air—have a very bad effect on the nails, some-

THE HAND

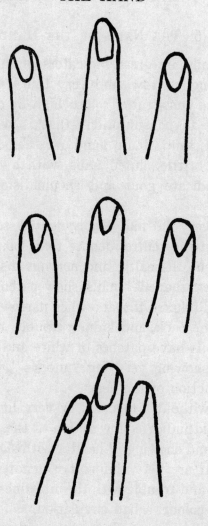

The Long Nails.

times turning them dark yellow and almost black.

Poisoning of any kind in the system appears to affect the nails : they get very dented and broken, turning brown and withering near the root.

To be in good health the nails should be naturally a rosy pink in colour, with a smooth shiny surface and a medium-sized " moon." The nails should be neither too long nor short, too narrow nor broad, but of medium length and size ; they will then indicate a good constitution and a normal disposition.

Short, broad nails announce irritability of the nervous system, being more inclined to worry than the long nails.

Long nails give an inclination to depression and melancholy, especially in bad health.

Very hard, round nails denote a tendency to paralysis.

White spots on red or fluted nails show there is uric acid in the blood—it is a warning of gout and rheumatism.

Broad pale nails with many prominent ridges will indicate a tendency to diabetes.

Puffy-looking hands with short red nails indicate internal health troubles—sometimes a tendency to dropsy—always a poor circulation, denoting chilblains and cramp.

THE HAND

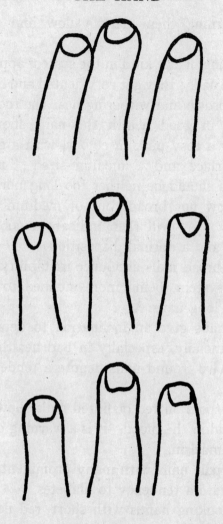

The Short Nails.

Shell-shaped nails indicate spinal and nerve illnesses.

(7) The Nails in Relation to the Temperament

The short, broad nails never give so even a temper as the long " filbert-shaped " nails— they announce a more irascible and easily " put out " nature, indicating that the critical faculties are developed with combativeness, often bestowing great courage and daring ; when they are also the strong red nails, with white spots, they denote cruel natures, especially on a hard thick hand.

Pale pink " filbert-shaped " nails show refinement and a sensitive nature, but with no great force of character.

Well kept round nails indicate a pleasure-loving and luxurious temperament ; if inclined to be red in colour, highly irritable.

Nails that are naturally very bright will give a quick and apprehensive mentality.

Very white short nails show the cynic ; long and pointed, sensitiveness and easily offended. Short nails are critical, taking little on trust.

Long nails are impressionable, understanding the intangible, being poetical and imaginative.

Big square, naturally bright, strong nails will give commercial and business abilities.

Very thin nails, with the tips bent inwards, will indicate a timorous, weak, and easily discouraged disposition ; and when having to face the adversities of life, becoming hopeless.

People with long nails are often weak and peevish in temperament.

With short nails they are irritable and impatient in manner ; when very short, discontent and a quarrelsome humour will be denoted.

THE INFLUENCE OF THE MOUNTS

PART NOW XI

THE INFLUENCE OF HUMAN RACES

THE INFLUENCE OF THE MOUNTS

(1)

THE palm of the hand is divided into three worlds—like the fingers.

At the base of each finger in the palm is to be seen a mount—this part of the hand represents the higher intelligence.

There are seven mounts of the hand that influence the destiny : the mounts of Jupiter, Saturn, the Sun or Apollo, Mercury, the Moon or Luna, Venus, and the two mounts of Mars.

The ancient cheirosophists named them after the planets and the characteristics of their gods. Thus the mount of Jupiter, which is found at the base of the first finger, when fairly developed indicates honour, noble ambition, religion, gaiety, will power, and a happy marriage. When in excess—that is, very high and invading the mount which is next to it—it will give excessive pride, love of power, a wish to rule, and a desire to shine, a domineering, self-assertive spirit. If absent it causes want of self-respect, indolence, vulgar tendencies.

The mount of Saturn is found immediately beneath the second finger—which the ancients assigned to Saturn, the planet of Fatality. It denotes a tendency to extremes in the fortune, either making it very good or very bad, depending on the signs and symbols written on this mount and the Line of Fate.

If this part of the hand is very prominent by the length of the finger or size and height of this mount, it will indicate a timid, remorseful nature, inclining to sadness and solitude, with little inclination for marriage. But when this mount is not over developed it will then give prudence, wisdom, and success, with a love of mysticism. The influence of Saturn gives a naturally cautious temperament—having to know one rather well before making a friendship, caring for so few, but unchanging in love and affection, though unforgiving in temper. The total absence of this mount indicates an insignificant life.

The mount of the Sun or Apollo is placed under the third finger, and signifies when well developed the love of all things beautiful—for he is the god of the Arts. It indicates talent for literature, sculpture, painting, or music ; often giving genius ; bringing glory and celebrity ; for he can confer great intelligence, with that serenity of soul that denotes a lovable and tolerant temperament, with grace and charm.

In excess it announces a great desire for riches and an extravagant love of show ; wearing much jewellery and expensive personal adornments— often in bad taste ; making the nature frivolous and boasting. If in total absence, a material, existence, with no appreciation of the Arts, culture or refinement ; a monotonous life, like a dreary winter's day without the sun.

The mount of Mercury is found under the little finger—dedicated to the beautiful " swift-winged messenger of the gods."

When well defined it gives great intelligence, with love of mental work, promptitude in thought and act, industry, activity of mind and body, eloquence of expression in speaking or writing. In excess it indicates cunning, impudence, theft, and falsehood ; under these attributes it was dedicated by the ancients to merchants, thieves, liars, and lawyers.

The absence of this mount will announce inaptitude for mental work, with little idea of the value of time ; making for unpunctuality.

Jupiter, Saturn, Apollo, and Mercury represent the spiritual gifts and the mentality.

The first mount of Mars is immediately under
the mount of Mercury—on the percussion of the
hand. It gives to the nature moral courage,
patience, devotion, and the power of resistance
to evil. In excess it denotes a martyr-like
nature, living the life that gives up everything
for an idea.

If absent it denotes impatience and a great
dislike for waiting for one's desires. This mount
well developed is more often found in the
woman's hands than the man's.

The second mount of Mars—to be seen inside
the Life Line under Jupiter—is more often developed in the man's hand and is often missing
in the woman's. It indicates physical courage
and daring ; if well developed it gives ardour
and resolution, with power of control over the
expression of temper and thoughts—a disci-
plined nature.

In excess, when rayed with lines and crosses,
it denotes anger, cruelty and revenge, a quarrelsome temper.

Its absence will indicate want of discipline in
expression of thoughts and temperament, often
giving cowardice when having to face dangers.
This part of the hand represents the World of

THE INFLUENCE OF THE MOUNTS

Action, these two mounts of Mars the natural and physical life, with its struggles, contests, work, endurance and labour.

The mount of Venus is found at the root of the thumb, occupying, with the mount of the Moon, the lower half of the palm of the hand, and together they represent the sensuous side of the life.

The mount of Venus, when fairly developed, indicates the love, sympathies, and emotions of the temperament, with appreciation of all things beautiful in form and colour ; melody in music, tenderness in affection, with a desire of being loved.

When in excess it gives too great a desire for material pleasures—making for inconstancy, sensuality, vanity, and idleness.

Its total absence indicates a want of love for humanity—coldness, egotism, without caring for the beautiful.

On the opposite side to the mount of Venus —the percussion of the hand—the mount of the Moon is seen, and when well developed it gives a romantic imagination, meditation, harmony in music, dreams, and interest in mysticism, also love of the sea, long journeys and changes.

In excess it indicates morbid melancholy,

caprice and discontent, restlessness, an unsettled nature.

If absent, little imagination; want of ideas; not caring for the romantic or poetical.

When these mounts are clearly indicated, but not too strongly defined, they will give the characteristics of the planet they represent; the counterfeit (the excess or total absence of the mounts) denoting a deformity in the temperament.

The significations of the mounts are augmented or greatly modified by the lines and the length or shortness of the fingers.

(2) CONCERNING THE UNION OF THE MOUNTS

Although the characteristics just described are those given by each mount, one dominating influence in the hands is rarely seen; more often there are two or three strong forces in the nature, either in harmony or discordant. It is for the cheiromantist to examine the hands and ascertain which is the dominating power.

The union of Saturn and Jupiter will give much thought and discrimination in public life or affairs. Jupiter and Apollo would give wisdom and justice, making for success in responsible positions.

The coalition of Mercury and Jupiter signalises the clever orator.

Saturn and Mercury allied indicates talent for business, with method and organisation ; making the temperament calculating and cautious ; if Mars is also in union it would add enterprise and energy.

Jupiter and Mars in union indicates clever soldiers ; and both allied with the Moon, sailors.

Mars and Mercury in concord gives quickness of thought and action, making the mind alert and witty.

Jupiter and Venus—the dominating mounts of the hand—in harmony indicates a love of riches and glory, giving brilliant, successful careers, with a liking for prominence, and desiring social success ; preferring to " set their light upon a hill to shine before all men," giving a humane nature and an agreeable temperament.

The union of Saturn and the Moon—the dominating influence—indicates one preferring the backwaters of life ; not being attached to the world of men ; more interested in ideas than the social or public life ; love of mysticism and country life ; being in accord with the spirit of nature.

Apollo and Luna most prominent indicates a

highly imaginative temperament, with talent for writing, and great appreciation of literature ; if Venus adds her influence it will give love of music and the arts.

Mercury, Saturn, and Luna in coalition denote interest in occultism, with clairvoyant powers ; the domestic life holding few attractions unless Venus is also in evidence.

Mars and Venus prominent will bring many romantic and passionate love affairs, but it does not indicate lasting affection.

The mount of Luna very dominant inclines the temperament to be romantic, dreamy, and unpractical ; with many ideas—rarely carried out owing to the changeability of the nature.

Mars and the Moon in alliance will signalize angry fits of temper ; and should Saturn add its influence it will then announce a very resentful nature, suspicious and unforgiving.

If Saturn and Mars are the dominant mounts in the hand it indicates a furious temper—especially on a thick, hard hand with a heavy thumb and short, broad, red nails—this being one of the criminal types.

Mercury, Venus, and Mars prevailing will give a vivacious and witty mind, good natured, with a gay and happy temperament, but inclined to inconstancy in love ; if with spatulate fingers, then it indicates talent for and a love of dancing.

If the mount of Apollo is the most dominant in the hand it denotes a daring, enterprising nature, always ready to play with chance and fortune. The mount of Saturn predominant indicates a tendency for the reverse—going to the extreme of caution, fear, and calculation.

Whichever of these mounts dominate in a hand it will indicate the ruling passion of the life, that is the natural and instinctive inclinations and desires of the temperament.

The Moon inclines one to day-dreaming—romance and caprice.

Mars denotes energy, impulse, passion, and temper.

Venus indicates appreciation of all things beautiful—love, tenderness, sensuous pleasures.

Mercury gives wit, quickness, and language.

Jupiter announces honour, pride, ambition, and authority.

Mercury, Jupiter, and Apollo when prominent will give a distinctive personality ; and whatever the position in life, in that sphere they will lead and rule.

BOOK II

ANCIENT PALMISTRY

" Each man's Fate is bound about his neck."
(Old Arab Saying.)

THE SEVEN PRINCIPAL LINES

1. THE LINE OF LIFE.
2. THE LINE OF HEAD.
3. THE LINE OF HEART.
4. THE LINE OF FATE OR OF SATURN.
5. THE LINE OF FORTUNE OR OF APOLLO.
6. THE LINE OF HEALTH OR HEPATIC LINE.
7. THE LINE OF INTUITION.

THE SEVEN PRINCIPAL LINES

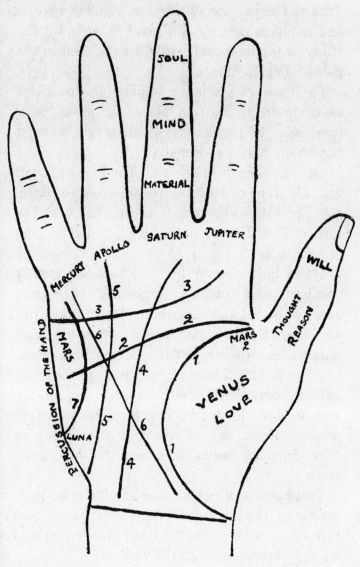

SOUL

MIND

MATERIAL

MERCURY APOLLO SATURN JUPITER

WILL

THOUGHT REASON

PERCUSSION OF THE HAND

MARS

MARS 2

VENUS LOVE

LUNA

G

THE HAND

THIS is the part of Cheiromancy which reveals and explains destiny, for good or evil, by the study of the lines and symbols to be seen in the palms of the hands.

To make this science intelligible one must understand, in the first place, the seven principal lines of the hand—which play the most important part in palmistry.

1st, The Line of Life.   2nd, The Line of Head. 3rd, The Line of Heart.   4th, The Line of Fate. 5th, The Line of Fortune or of Apollo.   6th, The Line of Health or Hepatic Line.   7th, The Line of Intuition.

These lines should be well formed, vividly coloured, and slightly luminous, with their quality noticed as to length, depth, and breadth, also their relative position to the other lines and mounts, as crossing, cutting, or touching them.

These principal lines of the hand are the foundation from which the past and present are known, and the future events of the life predicted.   From the diversity of their meaning these different names have been bestowed upon them.

These seven principal lines are the chief indicators of the life, character, love, fame, and fortune, as written on the hand and interpreted by the cheiromancy of the ancients.

THE SEVEN PRINCIPAL LINES

These lines should not be read consecutively, but understood in a correlative sense, as acting in conjunction with other signs and symbols.

These seven principal lines rarely change in character, but sometimes they vary in colour ; when dark and opaque they indicate worries, bad health, and disappointments ; if they have a luminous appearance it is always a fortunate sign, portending health, love, and successes.

Then there are the lesser lines to be considered —lines that are not always to be seen on the hand, developing sometimes quite unexpectedly, often indicating events of an important and interesting nature.

These lesser lines are :

1. The Influence Lines—relating to Love and Marriage.
2. The Children.
3. Voyages and Long Journeys.
4. The Line of Dissipation or Intemperance.
5. The Line of Mars.
6. Lines of Ambition.
7. The Girdle of Venus.
8. Enemies.
9. Solomon's Ring.
10. The Rascette or Magic Bracelet.

SECTION 1

THE LINE OF LIFE

1

THE LINE OF LIFE

"And the Lord God . . . breathed into his nostrils the breath of life : and man became a living soul."
Genesis, chap. ii.

WHEN this line is long and well formed, vividly coloured, completely surrounding the thumb, at the base of the mount of Venus, it will indicate a long life, free from serious illnesses, and conferring a happy temperament. When pale and broad it announces a tendency to bad health, evil inclinations, and an envious nature.

This line, broad, pale, and dark in colour, has always evil tendencies, either in health or character. If this Line of Life is broken on the left hand, but is marked in a continuous line on the right, it shows inherited weakness of constitution and danger of ill health, throughout a *fairly* long life. The other lines and mounts, with the nails and the Health Line, should be studied in reference to the illnesses threatened.

There is greater danger to the life if the broken line appears in both hands, and every care should be taken at that age corresponding with the place on the broken line.

If the lower branch of the cut line turns in towards the mount of Venus, there is not so much hope for the recovery of the health as when it bends towards the palm of the hand.

When the Line of Life is not clearly and finely cut, but is formed by chains or many small hair lines, it does not indicate a very strong constitution; sometimes this chained formation is only marked a little way on the Life Line. When the line recovers its normal condition it is a sign that at that age one will begin to get stronger and not be so susceptible to so many little illnesses; but as long as this chained formation lasts it will show delicate health—the Health Line and the shape of the hands and nails will indicate the part of the body that will cause the trouble.

When the Line of Life, instead of starting from the side of the thumb next to the first finger, throws out a strong branch line on to the mount of Jupiter, so that it would appear to rise from that mount, it indicates a desire for power; and if with a well developed thumb and good Head Line, it announces success to the ambitions, bringing honours and authority, high dignities and decorations.

When this formation of the Life Line is seen on the woman's hand it more often indicates gratification of her social ambitions ; but if a career is followed, conferring great successes. When the Life, Head, and Heart Lines are all joined together at the side of the hand, under the index finger, they portend misfortune, usually denoting danger of a violent or sudden death.

When the Life Line is not joined with the Line of Head, and there is a great empty space between the two lines, it indicates want of thought and intelligence about the affairs of life ; with other bad signs it will make for foolishness and untruthfulness, giving an envious nature. Should these two lines be red and broad it will denote cruelty, vanity, and love of money, often the life ending in a violent death. If these two lines are thick and hollow, being dark and red in colour, it gives to the nature wild passions.

A weak, slender Line of Life, very long, will denote danger of ill-health throughout the life. When the Line of Life is cut through by many little hair lines, looking like fine wrinkles, there are indicated maladies and illnesses.

A double line is sometimes—but rarely—seen forming a second Line of Life. This line is called the Line of Mars, as it commences from that mount and follows the Life Line in its course inwardly, repairing its breaks and defects. This Line of Mars confers much courage, and if a light red, success in a military career, giving great vitality and good health. In the woman's hand it indicates a very magnetic personality, conferring much fascination and the power of attraction, but not always bringing happiness; but the subject will be much loved of men or women, as the sex will determine.

These sister lines often repair the principal lines, but should both lines be broken or in a bad condition, then the disaster announced by them is serious ; but if both lines are equally good, then is signified equally good fortune. A narrow space between the Line of Life and the Line of Head will confer self-confidence, making for independence of criticism ; this formation is a help in public life.

The Line of Life when joined to the Line of Head indicates tact, giving careful consideration and thought about any work undertaken, often making the nature sensitive. It is not a helpful sign to have these two lines joined almost into the palm of the hand, for this indicates failure through a want of self-confidence, and with a long Saturn finger it announces timidity, apprehension, and fears; and only by very careful training in early life would one be able to combat these tendencies.

Many rays and crosses from the mount of Mars on to the Life Line indicates a bad temper and a sensual nature.

A black spot or dark dents on the Line of Life warns one of illness or some great misfortune affecting the health.

Lines crossing and cutting through the Life Line from the mount of Venus, and ending on the Head Line, denote illnesses from money worries or affairs, at that age when these lines cross the Life Line.

When the Line of Life throws branches upwards, and these branch lines are well formed and strong, passing through the plain of Mars, they denote that at the age they leave the Life Line there will be a new interest made successful through one's own efforts and personality, often attaining riches and honours.

A line rising upward from the Line of Life to the mount of Jupiter shows success by the subject's own abilities and developed talents. This line is seen in the hands of those who attain to the highest positions through their own

efforts—these lines making their appearance
often quite suddenly; and to whichever finger
these branches rise will indicate the channel of
success.

A line crossing the Life Line from the mount
of Venus, ending on the Heart Line, indicates
unhappiness in love and disappointed affections
at the age the line crosses the Life Line. When
these lines cross the Life Line from the mount
of Venus, it shows that others will make mischief and interfere in the life, bringing worries
and disappointments, and often unhappiness to
the affections. If these cross lines are irregular,
wavering, or forming islands across the hands,
then it indicates scandal and mischief. If one
of these lines are deeply scored, crossing the
hand to the mount of Mars, under Mercury, it
brings the danger of seduction, separation, or
divorce, these being imminent if there is a
corresponding island on the Fate Line.

All the lines that cross the Line of Life from
the mount of Venus are disappointments and
worries—the line or mount they pass to will
show the nature. When rayed, having the appearance of being cut into the mount of Venus,
they are portents of deep heart sorrows by the
neglect, faithlessness, or death of those much
loved; they are very unhappy signs relating to

the affections, for even the children pass out of the life, showing the parent little affection or sympathy.

If the Line of Destiny is broken by one of these lines, it signifies the death of near relations who have an important influence in the life ; sometimes it indicates loss of the marriage partner ; it always denotes great changes, bringing sorrows and sometimes personal dangers. Branch lines from the Life Line, running down the hand towards the mount of Luna, indicate voyages and journeys to foreign countries ; and should the Life Line end in a decided fork, it foreshadows long residence abroad, this being shown by a break in the Fate Line, which will also confirm the age when the change of country could be expected. Many fine hair lines falling down from the Life Line will indicate a nervous, delicate constitution.

A Line of Life that curves out into the palm of the hand gives great physical activity, determination, and a daring nature, with a strong constitution.

When the Line of Life lies close to the thumb there will be a want of physical energy and a timidity in the nature ; this formation of the Life Line does not indicate robust health.

A broken Line of Life portends illnesses ; if

broken in both hands at the junction of the Health Line, danger of death.

A Life Line ending in a small fork or with many lines falling denotes a want of vitality. Short deep lines or crosses cutting the Life Line are warnings of accidents or illnesses.

A Life Line curving out into the palm of the hand, long and brightly coloured, indicates that one would naturally live into old age, especially if this type of Life Line is seen in both hands.

If the left hand indicates good health, showing a long, clear, vivid Line of Life, also the Health Line free from evil signs and symbols relating to disease, maladies, or nerve strain, it denotes a naturally sound constitution and healthy life ; but if the right hand shows signs of bad health it denotes that bad health has been acquired by the mode of life, either through over-work that has been a strain on the nervous system, or sometimes through having to live in a country that is not congenial, or through carelessness or indiscretions, and is not natural. If these signs appear in the right hand it is a warning of coming ill health, if not taken in time.

If the left hand shows signs of bad health and the right hand improvement, developing a stronger Life Line, it denotes that great care has been taken of the health. It also indicates

THE LINE OF LIFE

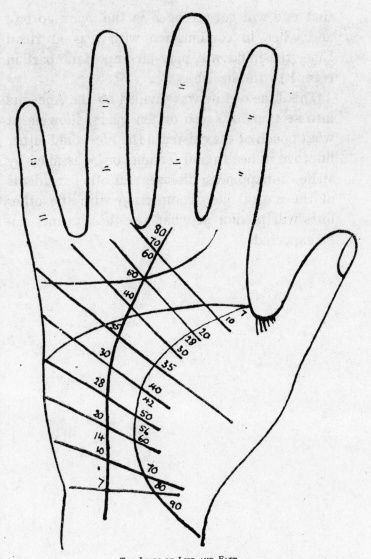

THE LINES OF LIFE AND FATE

divided into sevens and tens, making the centre of the palm of the hand thirty-five—
the first half of man's allotted span of life.

that one will get stronger as the years go on ; and when in combination with a good Head Line, the mind will play an important part in regard to the health.

This Line of Life was divided by the Ancients into sections of seven or ten years, showing at what epoch of the existence the life would either improve in health and fortune, or be assailed by strife, unhappiness, disease, and other incidents of the mortal life ; comparison with the other lines will predict at what age these events can be expected.

SECTION 2

THE LINE OF HEAD

2

THE LINE OF HEAD

" How noble in reason ! How infinite in faculty!
In apprehension, how like a god ! "—SHAKESPEARE.

THIS is the line from which one judges the character in its relation to the temperament, which is shown by the shape of the hand.

This Line of Head rises between the Line of Life and the first finger, at the base of the mount of Jupiter. When this line is long and clearly cut it will give sound judgment, a clever mind, with a good memory ; if crossing the hand and ending on the mount of Mars it denotes a strong will, with great determination.

The Line of Head very long and straight, extending across the hand, shows a disposition to be hard and avaricious, with an excess of calculation—always considering the personal advantages.

If the hand does not show a naturally strong

will by a long or broad " will " phalanx to the thumb, then this formation of the Head Line will indicate a development contrary to the temperament, through some unusual circumstances.

The Line of Head will often develop in this direction in a woman's hand after her marriage, showing that it has brought her great responsibilities in relation to the husband or children ; sometimes bringing a career for practical purposes, indicating the necessary development of realising the value of time and money, and often making for a strenuous life. If the Line of Head is long and drooping towards the mount of the Moon (which indicates the imagination), a less practical judgment of life is formed, and the ideal will take the place of realities.

With a very thin hand and long Saturn finger, this drooping formation of the Head Line makes the character inclined to be morbid and melancholy. When the Line of Head slopes to the mount of Luna in the left hand and is in a straight direction in the right it will indicate a great change to one's outlook on life through environment or circumstances, ideas which are not natural to the temperament.

A short, straight Head Line if deep and finely cut will give the power of mental concentration —but on one subject only, usually the career.

THE LINE OF HEAD

A long, slightly sloping Head Line will give understanding and interest in many ideas and pursuits, making the character sympathetic. A forked Head Line indicates the combination of practical reasoning abilities, with imagination and sympathy ; the branch that develops the stronger line will indicate the direction of the character. With a long little finger this type of Head Line gives diplomacy and tact, especially when joined to the Life Line at the beginning ; when there is a wide space between the two lines, with long flattened fingers, this type of Head Line announces lying and deceit.

The Head Line chained and islanded for some distance towards the middle of the hand indicates a want of concentration and slow development of the mental faculties ; if pale and faintly marked there is little self-confidence : it denotes hesitation and a lack of intelligence, making all study difficult.

When the Line of Head is not joined to the Line of Life at its starting point it makes for self-reliance, but at times over-impulsiveness. With the mount of Mars high and a long Jupiter finger it gives enthusiasm and boldness, with courage of opinions and audacity.

The Line of Head in touch with the mount of Mars gives an excitable mind, easily elated ; and if a branch of the Head Line falls towards the mount of Luna its possessor is quickly depressed·

When the Line of Head is serpentine in appearance it denotes a wavering character, with changes of opinion ; joined to the Life Line at the commencement, with a decided curve upwards, it will indicate a great gain of moral courage at that time. Should the Head Line throw a strong branch to one of the mounts, the mind turns towards those characteristics inspired by that mount. If to Mercury, and the hand shows talent for speaking or writing, it would indicate an interest in that direction ; if to the mount of Apollo, a love of art or a desire for riches. If to Jupiter, it inclines the nature to be ambitious, with a wish for authority ; to Saturn, the mind turns to agriculture and sometimes a business career.

When this Line of Head is broken immediately under the mount of Saturn it indicates a serious fatality ; if broken in both hands it announces the danger of a wound to the head that may prove fatal; if the break is only in the left hand it is a sign of inherited mental weakness.

A break in the Head Line, with the broken end sharply turning down, indicates a tendency to suicide. One of the old writers on this subject says : " Round knots, very red in colour, appearing on the Head Line show a tendency to commit murder."

Lines from the Head Line to the Heart Line announce many friendships, making for popularity and social success, indicating affection for and interest in one's friends.

A double Line of Head (which is rarely seen) —that is, another line closely following this principal line—bestows much talent and mental energy, a mind alert and active with many interests. Sometimes this mental energy is denoted as being beyond the physical strength ; it is then a warning against over-working— especially when seen on a hand that shows a delicate constitution. This double Line of Head on a woman's hand is often a sign of fortune by inheritance.

If the head and heart are represented by one line across the hand, it denotes a character that is difficult for most people to understand. This is another sign that is rarely seen—about one in two hundred—it is more often found in the hands of men who choose a military life for their careers, as it bestows a daring and courageous character, with love of an active life.

The Line of Head rising high on the Mount of Jupiter will indicate an ambitious mind, desiring power and authority ; if sloping down on to the Mount of Luna it gives sympathy and imagination, showing great ideals and ambition, sometimes for a cause or the welfare of others. But should this line go directly to the Mount of Mars on the percussion of the hand, it would make the desires more selfish and personal. It is these straight Lines of Head that " make the man selfish and the woman greedy."

The Line of Head turning up to the Mount of Mercury gives perspicuity, wit, quickness of thought and perspicacity—often to be seen on the hands of those who are famous for their histrionic talents and abilities—also making for social success, the mind being alert and gay. A long Head Line very much sloping to the Mount of Luna, with a wide space from the Life Line and a short " will " phalanx to the thumb, indicates an indolent mind, dreamy and un-practical ; if on a talented hand, then working only when very interested in the subject—denoting many moods and a changeable mind.

The straight Head Line gives greater mental energy. A broad, pale Head Line does not indicate great intelligence. This line should be finely and clearly cut, lightly coloured and a little luminous, starting from the Life Line, but not closely joined to it, slightly sloping towards the Mount of Luna as it crosses the palm of the hand ; it then announces a highly intelligent mind, with a good memory, learning rapidly and understanding readily.

When the Head Line is not normal in its formation—as being broken or in blocks, short and falling on to the Fate Line or Health Line, very dark in colour—it denotes extreme depression and anxiety. These signs were characteristic of young people's hands before and during the years of the Great War—foreshadowing the tragedy that most had to pass through. Islands, stars, and crosses are other unhappy signs, and should the Head Line be broken by these marks in both hands, then it portends death by accident, wars, or strife. Many small dark dots on the Head Line denotes mental fatigue, requiring more sleep than others to regain the vitality.

SECTION 3

THE LINE OF HEART

3

THE LINE OF HEART

UPON CUPID

"Love, like a gypsy, lately came,
And did me much importune,
To see my hand, that by the same,
He might foretell my fortune.

He saw my palm ; and then, said he :
'I tell thee, by this score here,
That thou, within few months, shalt be
The youthful Prince d'Amour here.'

I smiled and bade him once more prove,
And by some cross line show it,
That I could ne'er be Prince of Love,
Though here the princely poet."

HERRICK.

THE Line of Heart runs beneath the mounts, at the top of the palm of the hand.

When well coloured, deeply cut and straight, rising on the Mount of Jupiter, extending to the percussion of the hand, it signifies that its possessor has a good heart, a strong and fortunate love ; for one can judge of the strength and weakness of the attachments by the greater or less length of the Line of the Heart. If it does not rise until the Mount of Saturn, turning up sharply to that finger, then the love inclines rather to a sensual character, this type of Heart Line indicating strong physical passions. The Line of Heart extending over the Mount of Jupiter gives high ideals, so the love will be with a purer passion and less physically in-stinctive.

The Line of Heart stretching across the whole of the hand would give a passionate ideal, with constancy and loyalty in love, which often brings much suffering when giving this devotion to those who cannot appreciate a great affection.

When the Line of Heart is broken in many fragments it indicates inconstancy both in love and friendship; the old writers say, " Contempt of women too." These breaks in the line often denote organic weakness of the heart : if broken under the Mount of the Sun and this break occurs in both hands, it may prove a fatal ill-ness ; if breaking under the Mount of Saturn, it announces a tragic end to the love ; fickleness, folly, and flirtations to satisfy the vanity are indicated by these many breaks in the Heart Line. If under the Mount of Mercury, the unhappy end of the love will be from caprice.

When this Line of the Heart appears in the form of a chain, with many little hair lines instead of one clear line, it indicates inconstancy with many empty flirtations rather than a deep and lasting love ; passing round the percussion to the back of the hand it gives jealousy. An ardent passionate love nature is indicated by a deep red Heart Line ; but when pale and wide it is a sign of indifference.

Should the Line of Heart droop towards the Line of Head and touch it, it denotes great disappointment to the affections, and is one of the signs of widowhood. The Heart and the Head Lines close together as they cross the hand announces many prejudices, with narrow ideas, being difficult temperaments to live with ; their love is exacting, having one point of view for themselves but quite a different one for others.

A Heart Line forked on the Mount of Jupiter makes a loyal and faithful friend. Bright red or black spots on this line show illnesses of the heart.

When strong lines cut through the Heart Line by other than the principal lines, these intersections bring many misfortunes and disappointments to the affections. Branch lines reaching

out on to the mounts will announce the strong
attractions of the characteristic given by the
mount ; if these lines go to Mercury it gives the
love of writing or speaking ; to the Mount of
the Sun on a conical hand, a love of the artistic ;
if the square hand, desire for riches ; to the
Mount of Saturn, appreciation of personal
comfort.

The Heart Line long, rising between Jupiter
and Saturn, bestows a loving disposition, with
almost too much devotion, self-sacrificing in
either work or affection. Jealousy in love is
shown by the Heart Line lying close up to the
mounts ; but if very long and passing round the
percussion of the hand, it gives an intensity to
the passional nature that under provocation
makes for violence.

Ideal love is shown when the Heart Line rises
on the Mount of Jupiter. If the loved one does
not reciprocate these devotions, then feeling the
disappointment keenly; these long idealistic
lines bring many heart-aches. A jagged appearance of the Heart Line shows inconstancy with
petty intrigues, a series of attachments, but
never giving a deep or lasting love. A Heart
Line bare and without branches will give a
cold, unsympathetic and unemotional nature.
White spots on the Heart Line signify love in-

trigues. A hand without this Line of the Heart indicates bad faith and an iron will—a wicked nature. Pale broad lines mark the profligate. The deep red lines give passion to the love. The long Heart Line shows the idealistic love. The Heart Line short, indicates love of a more physical nature, and if broken, jagged, chained, or with islands, it will denote inconstancy, love intrigues, many affairs of the heart, and selfishness.

The Heart and Head combined in one line across the hand rarely brings happiness in love, making the temperament difficult for others to live with or understand. Should this line cross the hand from the Mount of Mars to the percussion, it indicates cruelty and hardness, but often much courage and daring—generally an unusual character. This is one of the signs not often seen in a hand.

SECTION 4

THE LINE OF FATE OR OF SATURN

4

THE LINE OF FATE OR OF SATURN

" There is a tide in the affairs of men, which
Taken at the flood leads on to fortune."
SHAKESPEARE.

THIS Line is Fatality, and shows the Destiny.

Rising to the Mount of Saturn and crossing it to the base of the middle finger, there are four points from which it may start : the Mount of Luna, the Rascette at the wrist, the Line of Life, or from the Plain of Mars.

When this line is seen rising up from the Mount of Luna and passing to that of Saturn it indicates the influence and affection of another over the fate, placing one's fortunes and success at the caprice of others, making one a child of Fate—sometimes " Those who have greatness thrust upon them."

Desbarrolles says : " There are people really happy and fortunate by fatality."

When the Fate Line begins from the wrist

immediately below the finger of Saturn, going in a direct line, tracing a deep furrow in that mount but stopping at the base of the finger, it is a sign of great good fortune, indicating a destiny to which is given the desirable things of this world. This is more often seen in the hands of " those who are born great." When it cuts through the base of the finger of Saturn and mounts to the third phalanx it portends to a great destiny either good or evil—for it is then excessive fatality.

If this Line of Saturn rises from the Life Line it indicates the power to shape or mould the destiny more as one would wish it to be, good fortune then coming through personal merit and developed talents, showing much determination—" those who achieve greatness."

When starting from the Plain of Mars it signifies difficulties and obstacles to success in the early life; sometimes slow development of the personality; but if straight and well coloured at its termination, crossing the Mount of Saturn, it will indicate success and contentment in the second half of the life, after struggles and disappointments in the early years.

When the Fate Line is straight, with many branches rising up to the other mounts, it then announces passing from poverty to affluence.

THE LINE OF FATE

If the Fate Line stops at the Line of Head it portends misfortune through wrong calculations —the judgment cannot be relied upon ; if other parts of the hand indicate bad health, it would show a physical defect of the brain.

A very broken or irregular Fate Line denotes a life with many troubles and worries, especially when broken on the Head Line. The breaks occurring near the Heart Line bring unhappiness through the affections ; if the Line of Life or Health shows a delicate constitution, breaks on the Fate Line often refer to illnesses. Lines falling from this Saturnian Line bring losses and difficulties through the treachery of others.

All lines cutting the Fate Line show sorrows and vexations in either health, love, or money —these cross lines being the opposing influences in the life.

When fine lines are to be seen leading upwards, or almost parallel with the Fate Line, making for the Line of Heart, it will indicate marriage at that date at which the line leaves or touches the Fate Line. These fine lines that are seen near this Saturnian Line represent those who are attracted.

Breaks on the Fate Line always announce important changes in the life.

This Line of Fate does not always go direct

to the finger of Saturn : it will be seen sometimes rising up to the other mounts. If its course is towards Jupiter it will bring into the life satisfied ambitions and power ; when to the Mount of Apollo, it brings riches and celebrity or success in an artistic or literary career, the shape of the hand showing the temperament and so the desires—proceeding through life according to one's type, which is the occult law that one obeys. When mounting up to Mercury it gives an interest in commerce or scientific pursuits, indicating talent for speaking or writing, making these influences prominent in the life.

A twisted or wavering Fate Line indicates troubles and anxieties ; and until this line becomes straight and direct the life will be full of difficulties ; if very faintly marked it denotes an uneventful existence.

A double or sister Fate Line, which is sometimes seen close to the principal line and clearly marked, signifies material advantages and improving affairs generally ; but should these double Fate Lines start from different points in the hand, one line running from the Life Line and the other rising from the Mount of Luna, it indicates a strange and undesirable fate, bringing a tendency to moral corruption, with great love of material pleasures, portending nothing permanent or tangible, pursuing always shadows and myths in fortune and happiness. When seen with a Head Line much apart from the Life Line, then it denotes a sensual and stupid outlook on life, living on expectations that lead to a cul-de-sac.

Influence Lines running from the Life Line at the base of the thumb to the Fate Line show the parents' influence. Should they cross this Line of Fate in heavy strokes it indicates great unhappiness through one's own family, and their interference and misunderstanding of one's temperament; but when these lines run parallel with the Fate Line it will then indicate sympathy and help from one's own people.

These fine Influence Lines accompanying the Fate Line up the hand to the mounts between the Fate and the Life Line are a great help and support, as they are bonds of love with near relations.

Should one of these Influence Lines be stronger than the Fate Line it shows that the early life is overshadowed by a stronger personality—often one of the parents. A line from the root of the thumb in the left hand will indicate a step-parent : the nature of the line will show whether the influence is an unhappy one.

SECTION 5

THE LINE OF FORTUNE OR OF APOLLO

5

THE LINE OF FORTUNE OR OF APOLLO

" And in thy majesty ride prosperously."
Psalm xlv.

THIS is sometimes called the Line of the Sun, and when seen rising from either the Line of Life or the Mount of Luna and tracing a furrow in the Mount of Apollo, straight and well defined, it signifies success and celebrity in literature or art—whether in poetry, painting, music, or sculpture—the mounts deciding which branch of the arts is preferred. Venus inclines to music and colour, and the Mount of Luna to literature.

The Line of Apollo strongly traced on the hand, even if one does not follow art as a career, denotes that one will receive from that line the desire and appreciation of beautiful things. If seen on a practical, useful hand, it will then give a great wish for riches, and for success to one's labours and career.

When this line is straight, long, and clear,

cutting deeply into the Mount of Apollo, it will announce a passion for riches and fame. This line strongly traced on the hand will always give a great desire for celebrity, riches, and glory ; and if more evident than the Fate Line, life will be full of risks and excitement in the pursuit of this " Goddess of Fame and Victory " without the stability and foundation to the fortunes as when given by a decided and strong Fate Line. When this Line of Fortune is seen on a talented hand with a clear Head Line it confers a brilliant pathway through life—successes and riches, easily attained.

This line rising on the Mount of Luna will give the power of expression in the artistic world —showing there is inherent the creative force. But when this line rises only from the Heart Line, then the artistic power is only appreciative and not productive.

When the Line of Apollo in its upward course is intersected by many lines, these indicate the obstacles to the success of the career ; but if this Sun Line continues, marked as a deep and single line making a decided furrow as it passes through the mount rising to the finger, these obstacles will eventually be overcome and fame and riches will be attained. If the Line of the Sun has many branches when crossing its mount, all going in different ways, it is then power neutralised by division—which does not make for success.

But these lines equally deep and entirely of the same strength and power, rising to the finger of Apollo, making deep furrows as they cross the mount, it will bring glory, fame, and riches. This Line of the Sun deep and very clear indicates the friendship and favour of the great.

Lines barring and cutting through the Line of Apollo announce obstacles and envy, and often the disapproval and disfavour of those in power. An Island on this line is loss of one's good name and reputation.

A Triangle will give skill in scientific art— medicine, engineering, architecture.

A Star portends loss of fortune, but beyond one's power to prevent.

THE LINE OF HEALTH OR HEPATIC LINE

THE LINE OF HEALTH OR HEPATIC LINE

" Disease is fear made manifest on the physical Body."
The Science of Mind-healing.

THIS line usually rises either from the wrist or the Line of Life, and goes in the direction of the Mount of Mercury.

It should be straight, long, well coloured, and not too broad, for then it indicates good health, a retentive memory, and success in business affairs.

When cut or broken, marked like a spiral or undulating, it indicates digestive weakness, stomach trouble, denoting that care should be taken about diet ; when dark in colour this line shows internal illness—if a dark red a tendency to disease and feverish complaints. When this line is well formed and of good colour it gives a bright and joyous spirit, carrying one through all difficulties.

When the Health Line forms a triangle with

the Line of Fate and the Line of Head it gives intuition and an aptitude for magic.

This Hepatic Line, when seen rising to the Mount of Mercury and free from intersection of all kinds, bestows good health to old age ; but should it become broken, forked, or forming islands, then it shows the danger of severe illness.

When seen rising out of the Life Line, and ending or deeply cutting the Head Line, illnesses of the head are indicated ; and when a deep red in colour, there is danger of apoplexy. Stopping with a dot or star on the Heart Line, and the lines unequally coloured, shows weakness of the heart's action. Forming a large cross with the Line of Head it gives an inclination for the study of the occult sciences. If an arrow cuts the Line of Health, forming a small cross, it signifies a coming illness, with the danger of a surgical operation.

It is a better sign for the health when this line does not touch the Line of Life and is seen running down the hand towards the Rascette ; it then promises a long life free from disease.

Crossing the hand to the Mount of Luna it denotes a capricious nature—restless as the sea.

The Line of Health broken and red gives an angry temper, poisoning the blood ; bilious and feverish attacks when broad and dark in colour.

THE LINE OF HEALTH

An island on this line indicates internal weaknesses and organic trouble.

It is a sign of a robust constitution not to have this line on the hand. When it cuts through the Line of Life it indicates that the health is undermining the life, and the age at which the two lines meet is the point of death.

SECTION 7

THE LINE OF INTUITION OR
PRESENTIMENT

7

THE LINE OF INTUITION OR PRESENTIMENT

" As when with downcast eyes we muse and brood,
And ebb into a former life, or seem
To lapse far back in some confused dream
To states of mystical similitude ;
If one but speaks or hems or stirs his chair,
Ever the wonder waxeth more and more,
So that we say : ' All this hath been before,
All this hath been, I know not when or where.'
So, friend, when first I look'd upon your face
Our thoughts gave answer each to each, so true—
Opposed mirrors each reflecting each—
That tho' I knew not in what time or place
Methought that I had often met with you,
And either lived in either's heart and speech."

TENNYSON.

THIS line often takes a curved form, appearing almost in a semicircle—it is a line not often seen in the hands.

When rising on the Mount of Mercury and passing to the Mount of Luna, with these mounts high, and in combination with a long Saturn finger, it portends vivid and reliable intuition.

If clearly marked in both hands it then indicates psychic powers, giving a love of mysticism and divination. It is not a fortunate line to possess in an ordinary sense, for it brings trouble with past incarnations, usually unhappy psychological ties and soul debts to be paid.

When found entwined with the Health Line it denotes illnesses—more of the emotions or soul than actually of the physical body, acting and reacting on one another; the only cure in these cases is through " spiritual healing." It bestows mediumistic powers and clairvoyance, the faculty of prevision and the authority of prescience. This is the line that relates to the Karmic past.

SECTION 8

THE LESSER LINES

THE LESSER LINES

1. THE INFLUENCE LINES RELATING TO LOVE AND MARRIAGE.
2. THE CHILDREN.
3. VOYAGES AND LONG JOURNEYS.
4. THE LINE OF DISSIPATION OR INTEMPERANCE.
5. THE LINE OF MARS.
6. LINES OF AMBITION.
7. THE GIRDLE OF VENUS.
8. ENEMIES.
9. SOLOMON'S RING.
10. THE RASCETTE OR MAGIC BRACELET.

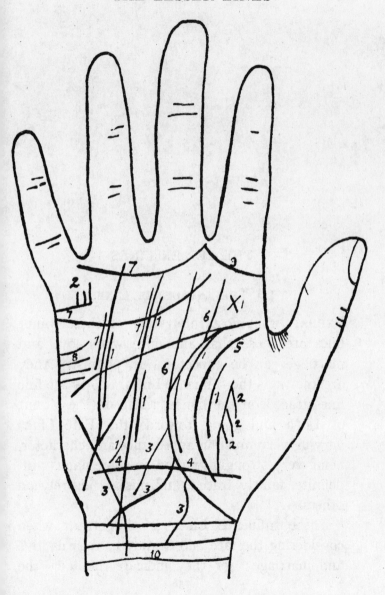

8

THE LESSER LINES

(1) THE INFLUENCE LINES

PERHAPS the most interesting of these minor lines are those that announce when love and marriage can be expected. In palmistry they are known as the Influence Lines. They are fine lines traced on the hands, rising on the Mount of Luna and going towards the Fate Line; varying very much in appearance and character, being very strongly marked on some hands; indefinite, faintly traced, and missing entirely on others.

These Influence Lines are important when considering the fate and destiny as regards love and marriage; for they indicate the age "the attractions " come into the life and what effect they will have on the fate. When one of these Influence Lines rises up to and unites with the Fate Line, then follows that line in its course; and the Sun Line deepens or begins with one of these fine Influence Lines; also the Line of Marriage on the Mount of Mercury is free from crosses, islands, and is unbroken—then can be expected a fortunate and successful marriage, at that time of the life when the Influence Line touches the the Line of Fate.

Should there also be an Influence Line, straight and distinct, on the Mount of Venus, closely following the Life Line at the same age as indicated by the influence to the fate—when these signs are seen on the hands it denotes the coming of one who is an affinity, which means an ideal and harmonious union of love and understanding.

These are the most powerful significations for a marriage that will be blissful, happy, and successful.

A well-made cross on the Mount of Jupiter is a symbol which denotes satisfaction in having accomplished the union, and also indicates that one great love will come into the life. Should these Influence Lines be definitely marked on the right hand and only faintly traced on the left, then the love and interest is on the other

side—the one attracted. But when only deeply
marked on the left, the marriage is uncertain,
but desired; for it is a sign of cross purposes
without unity or agreement in love.

Small lines barring the Influence Lines denote obstacles and interference; sometimes they
relate to the character of the one attracted;
crosses or stars on these lines are portents of
evil, worry, and shocks.

Pythagoras said : " Human nature is represented by the straight and crooked line."

These Influence Lines serpentine or islanded
indicate bad health or loss of money of the fiancé,
also bringing attacks on the character. Should
one of these Influence Lines cut through the
Fate Line, it will denote a broken engagement.

The Marriage Line on the Mount of Mercury
forked, jagged, or islanded, will indicate unhappy
love affairs and disappointed affections after
marriage.

When the Influence Line on the Mount of
Venus is seen turning up the mount away from
the Life Line it indicates changing affection and
faithlessness of the lover or husband. When
these Influence Lines within the Life Line on
the Mount of Venus are forked, uncertain and
weak, it will bring unhappy attachments. But
when they lie close to the Life Line, even, long,

and free from interceptions of every kind, then it indicates a mutual and happy love. The Mercury Marriage Line falling on to the Heart Line, and a line falling from the Heart Line under the Mount of Jupiter to the Head Line, will bring heart sorrows, and is one of the signs of widowhood—signalised at that time in the life when there is to be seen a break on the Fate Line.

A looped or islanded line from the Mount of Venus, crossing the Life Line and touching the Fate Line, warns one of an adverse influence bringing loss, worry, and great unhappiness ; it is also one of the signs of seduction.

When a line rises from Mars inside the Life Line crossing to the Mercury Marriage Line, this portends serious disagreements and trouble to the marriage, often ending in divorce.

These Influence Lines contain much history, requiring intuition and mental concentration on their minute details before one can rely on accuracy in reading them.

All these fine, oblique or parallel lines near the Fate Line, on either side, will indicate " the attractions " and the influence of others over one's fate and fortune.

The Influence Lines on the Life Line side of the Fate Line refer to one's own near relations, or friendships of one's own sex, the length of the line showing its duration ; on the percussion or Luna side of the Fate Line, then representing the love affairs of those met in the outer world, as one passes through life. When these Influence Lines turn away from the Fate Line, or those on the Mount of Venus from the Life Line, after being strongly marked and approaching, it is an unhappy sign, portending the loss of that friend, either by indifference or far distance. Marriages taking place late in life are often indicated by a break in the Fate Line, showing a complete change in the destiny.

A strong and clear Influence Line running parallel with the Fate Line or on Venus, near the Life Line, will announce the coming love and devotion of another at the age it first appears near the Life or Fate Line. If near the Fate Line on the side near the Life Line, it indicates a near relation or friendship ; on the other side of the Fate Line, then denoting the lover or husband, always the opposite sex.

Often to be seen are still finer lines, rising out of these Influence Lines, throwing branches to the different mounts of the hand : these finer hair lines relate to the fortunes of the fiancé, and much can be foretold from them.

When the following four signs of marriage are clearly marked on the hands, namely, the influence to the fate, the well-made small cross on Jupiter, the Marriage Line on the Mount of Mercury, and also the Influence Line on the Mount of Venus, then is foretold an exceptionally fortunate and happy marriage with an affinity. An affinity means an ideal companionship and friendship. Occultists say " we have seven affinities and one twin soul ; " the twin soul is more often on higher planes than the earth. The consciousness of this adoring love can only be realised through the spiritual imagination that is so often dormant in the sub-conscious mind. The death of the physical body sometimes brings the union with the twin soul, but it depends on whether we have reached those high vibrations, for element goes to element. As night cannot blend with day, so good and evil can never be one.

> " There to wander far away,
> On from island unto island at the gateway of the day."
>
> TENNYSON.

(2) CHILDREN

Rising on or near the Line of Marriage on the Mount of Mercury will be seen small perpendicular lines. These represent the children. If there are no lines to be seen on this mount, with a star or island on the Health Line, it is often a sign that there will be no children of the marriage. But with the Mount of Venus high, and many of these small lines on the Mount of Mercury, it indicates a tendency to have a family. The strongly marked lines announce more often boys and the finer lines girls.

These lines rising from the Line of Heart indicate great love of children, especially with the Mounts of Saturn and Venus well developed ; it will then indicate greater love for the children than the husband or wife, whichever sex it is.

If these lines start away from the Heart Line or Marriage Line it would show the nature of the children to be independent and not devoted to the parent. Slanting lines will show more sympathetic and sensitive natures in the children. These lines should be long, clear, and decidedly marked, indicating strong, healthy, clever children, giving the parent little trouble in their upbringing. Islands, stars, dots or crosses have the same meaning on these lines as in other parts of the hand.

A very decided line cutting through these lines on Mercury will indicate that the children will predecease the parent.

When the Marriage Line is also strongly marked on the Mount of Venus it shows the union to be one of love ; the children are often marked rising out of this Influence Line. These lines indicating the children are always clearer in the woman's hand than the man's, unless he has an uncommonly paternal nature. The success of the children's careers will often be entwined in the mother's Fate and Sun Lines; the boys are much more likely to take after the mother's side of the family in temperament and mentality, the girls the father's; but the eldest child always has a strong likeness to the father, not only in appearance but also in temperament. Where there is a clever man there has been a clever mother!

Often the coming of the child is to be seen in the mother's hand; it is heralded by a minute electric spark, which a great scientist said he " found at the beginning of all life."

(3) TRAVELLING AND VOYAGES

A decided and wide fork on the Life Line will indicate that the career will be away from the place of birth; and should the outer lines cross the hand towards the Mount of Luna it denotes a great change of country—sometimes meaning one was born in another land. A long line running up the hand from the Rascette to the Mount of Mercury would signify a great success coming into the life abroad.

These long lines mounting up to the Fate and Sun Lines from the percussion of the hand will show that the success of the life will be abroad —that it is one's fate and destiny to leave the native country and live for years in a far-off land.

When clear and deeply marked, uncrossed or unbroken, without islands, stars, or dots, the journeys are pleasant and successful. In a woman's hand they are often brought into her life by marriage ; in a man's, by his career.

(4) THE LINE OF DISSIPATION
OR INTEMPERANCE

When this line appears in both hands, with a small thumb and a weak sloping Head Line, with the little finger bent or crooked, or a long finger of Saturn and the Girdle of Venus, there will be a decided inherited tendency to dissipation, debauchery, and drink, with also the Mounts of Venus and the Moon in excess.

When strongly marked in the left hand only, cutting through the Fate Line, it signifies an adverse fate in the early life through the intemperance of one of the parents—in a woman's hand, as a rule the father ; and this tendency would have to be watched in her own sons.

Stars or islands on this line show that dissipation will often be the cause of death.

But on a hand with a strong thumb and good Head Line this tendency is kept well under control.

(5) THE LINE OF MARS

This line forms a second Line of Life, following it in its course inwardly from the Mount of Mars. Branches parting from this line and crossing the Mount of Mars, gives violent emotions through its excess of ardour.

It announces great success in all combats and fights, in military life or civilian. Branch lines extending over the Mount of Mars, rising high on the Mount of Jupiter, indicates riches and honours after trials and difficulties, often law-suits.

Small black holes or red crosses on this Line gives a violent temper—that might commit murder in a fit of passion. Lines setting out from the Mount and Line of Mars, attacking the Life Line, signify wounds. This Line of Mars gives strength and vitality, with great powers of physical endurance.

This line strongly marked and red gives physical attraction and fascination — passionate devotion in love.

(6) THE LINES OF AMBITION

These lines mounting to the fingers from the Life Line indicate in which direction the ambitions will be successful. They always announce that at the time they leave the Line of Life greater responsibilities will have to be taken up.

When these lines are straight, clear, and direct, unbarred and uncrossed, they then signify the realisation of one's ambitions.

But if broken, barred and crossed, the ambitions, wishes, and desires are disappointed— bringing unhappiness and an adverse fate. Sometimes they indicate in a man's hand the age at which he will marry; showing the responsibilities the marriage will bring, advancing his career and making for success, especially when these lines rise towards the Mount of Saturn. The wife will then play an important part in reference to his success. These lines on a hand are always an indication of ambition, either in marriage or the career.

(7) The Girdle of Venus

This was not considered by the ancients a good or fortunate line to possess. It is not seen in many hands, but if found on a thick palmed hand with a high Mount of Venus and a small supple thumb it would signify debauchery and physical passions that ruled the nature.

THE LESSER LINES

When this Girdle of Venus is seen on a soft hand with a long Saturn finger, and a high Mount of Luna, it is a sign of hysteria and high tension of the nervous system—giving eccentricity and depraved tastes.

These bad signs are modified when this Girdle of Venus is found on a clever hand with a powerful Head Line and strong thumb.

The Girdle of Venus on a soft hand with a small or pointed thumb and a long Line of Heart, chained, jagged, or full of little islands, will indicate perverted attachments and eroticism. Running into the Line of Marriage on Mercury it makes the nature exacting and difficult to please in the married life.

(8) ENEMIES

Enemies are shown by many lines cutting through the Fate and Sun Lines; also if the Mount of Mars under Mercury is much rayed with fine lines, showing one lives in an uncongenial environment of bickering, arguments, and tempers. The stronger these lines appear the more serious the quarrels; if in the shape of small islands rising up to the Fate or Sun Lines they will often indicate law-suits; if these lines end in crosses or stars there is physical danger from these enemies.

THE HAND

It is always better to get away from the influence or environment which causes these lines to deepen and grow, as they indicate so little rest or peace in the daily life while they remain.

(9) SOLOMON'S RING

This line is to be seen encircling the root of the first finger—Jupiter. It is rarely found on a hand but is supposed to confer wisdom, good judgment, balance and poise, with a straight and upright character.

(10) THE RASCETTE OR MAGIC BRACELET

These are lines drawn at the juncture of the hand to the wrist, forming a bracelet. When these three lines are prominent and deeply scored —without wrinkles or breaks—it signifies good fortune and a long life with tranquillity and happiness.

When lines from this bracelet rise on to the Mount of the Moon it indicates many journeys. If a strong and clear line rises from the Rascette, crossing the Plain of Mars and arriving on the Mount of Apollo, it presages riches and honour coming from the unexpected favour of those in power. A line direct from this bracelet to the little finger indicates much travelling.

THE LESSER LINES

A line rising from the Rascette near the percussion of the hand, cutting through the Mount of Luna and entwining in the Health Line, brings adversities and tribulations, and often bad health.

One of the old writers on this subject says :

" If a cross is found in the middle of the wrist lines it is the clasp of the bracelet, denoting a life destined to labour ; but endowed at last with an inheritance or unexpected gain."

These seven principal lines to be seen on the palm of the hands, more or less deeply engraven, broken or unbroken, softly or strongly coloured, making broad or narrow furrows, also these lesser lines with their infinite variety, are the markings of the sub-conscious self—still so great a mystery. The ancients considered these symbols heaven's own hieroglyphics, and there is no harm in trying to read them.

It is a natural law that shapes the hands, and by their comparison one assigns certain characteristics to them ; for truth comes to light by observation, and understanding by mental induction—just as the most casual observer could see there is a difference between the race-horse and the cart-horse in formation and temperament.

THE HAND

The form or appearance of the many lines is a symbol of the events signified ; for example, a broken or islanded Heart Line would indicate broken engagements and empty flirtations. A pale and badly formed Life Line—denoting a want of vitality, a frail life.

SECTION 9

RELATING TO THE SIGNS AND SYMBOLS

SIGNS AND SYMBOLS

1. THE STAR.
2. THE CHAINED LINE.
3. THE FORKED LINE.
4. THE FEATHERED LINE.
5. THE ISLAND.
6. THE BARRED LINE.
7. THE BROKEN LINE.
8. THE SQUARE, OR MARK OF PRESERVATION.
9. THE SPOT OR POINT.
10. THE CROSS.
11. THE CIRCLE.
12. THE SMALLER TRIANGLE.
13. THE GRILLE.

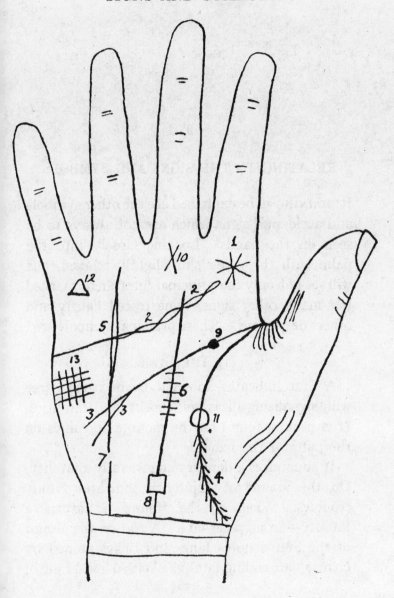

RELATING TO THE SIGNS AND SYMBOLS

REMAINING to be explained are the other symbols and accidental signs which are not always to be seen on the hands. Looking closely into the palm with the outer skin slightly relaxed, one will see not only the principal lines there marked but many other signs, some traced lightly and others deeply cut. These principal symbols are :

(1) THE STAR

A Star indicates an event beyond one's free will, signalising disasters, shocks, and fatalities. It is usually found on the mounts and lines on the palm of the hand.

It announces a danger and generally a fatality. On the Mount of Jupiter it indicates family troubles. When on the Mount of Saturn, a fatality—an adverse fate. A star on the Mount of the Sun denotes fame and riches gained by chance, but ending fatally. With a good Line of the Sun on a talented hand a star on this line will denote a great talent, bringing success and fame. Three parallel lines and a star on the Mount of the Sun signalises riches.

A star on the Mount of Mercury denotes deceit and fraud.

A star on the Mount of Mars under Mercury foreshadows assassination or the danger of a violent death. On the Mount of Mars under Jupiter inside the Life Line it will indicate law-suits, strife, and difficulties. When on the Plain of Mars there is the danger of loss or accidents by travelling, or sometimes earthquake.

A star on the Mount of the Moon announces danger from water ; if on the Health Line an illness that will necessitate a surgical operation.

A star on the Mount of Venus means disappointed affection ; on an Influence Line, danger or illness of a much-loved friend. On the Life Line, severe illness ; if in both hands, danger of sudden death. On the Head Line, shock or accident to the head, causing mental trouble and sometimes blindness. On the Heart Line it indicates trouble and loss, bringing great unhappiness in love.

When a star is seen on the Triangle it brings poverty and an adverse fate.

On the Quadrangle it indicates loss of a friend by deception.

(2) THE CHAINED LINE

The Chained Line indicates struggles, losses, obstacles, loneliness, and opposition of every kind.

(3) THE FORKED LINE

The Forked Line is usually found at the beginning or end of a line, denoting exuberance, and adding power to any line upon which it is placed, except the Life Line ; when there it indicates loss of vitality, a poor constitution.

(4) THE FEATHERED LINE

The Feathered Line indicates a weakness of that line.

(5) AN ISLAND

An Island is formed by a line dividing and then joining, and not by cross lines. It is an evil sign and brings much trouble. When seen on the Health Line on or near the Mount of Luna it will refer to the health, bringing danger of internal disease, cancer, tumours. If on this line and close to the Mount of Mercury it indicates loss by fraud and deceit, leading to bankruptcy.

SIGNS AND SYMBOLS

Many small islands on the Life Line if in both hands show inherited weakness of constitution, and while these islands last there will be a tendency to ill health and want of vitality. Islands on the Head Line will sometimes indicate trouble and weakness of the sight, these islands showing in childhood ; the eyes should not be strained and the mental capacity not over-worked.

The Heart Line with many islands, and short nails with large moons or no moons, will indicate inherited organic heart disease ; but an isolated island denotes a long unhappy attachment, often ending in disappointment.

An island on the Fate Line is always an un-fortunate period of the life, bringing losses and anxiety ; if an Influence Line touches this symbol it indicates that at that time of one's life there will be an unhappy attachment. On the Line of the Sun it will often indicate a lonely life and anxiety about money and one's possessions.

On the Marriage Line under Mercury or on any of the Influence Lines an island will announce sorrow, illness, or loss of the loved one. Islands crossing the principal lines of the hands show the adverse influences that bring moral temptation ; these signs are warnings, indicating dangers of a fatal or disgraceful nature, with loss of one's reputation if there is a corresponding Island on the Sun Line.

(6) THE BARRED LINES

The Barred Lines announce obstacles and misfortunes.

(7) THE BROKEN LINE

The Broken Line indicates opposing accidents.

(8) THE SQUARE

A Square denotes power, giving good sense and coolness in danger, being a symbol of preservation from accident or illness. A square near a star or other sign of danger signifies one will escape or recover. A broken square on Venus, if on a weak or unfortunate hand, is a warning of seclusion or imprisonment.

(9) THE SPOT OR POINT

A Spot or Point in the lines implies wounds.

A white point on the Heart Line, love intrigues.

A black spot on the Head Line will show nerve illnesses and mental fag with depression, sometimes deafness.

A red point or spots, danger of wounds.

A black spot on the Life Line indicates serious illness.

(10) A Cross

A Cross is found independent of the lines and not made by them. An uneven, badly formed cross is an unfavourable sign. On the Mount of Mercury it shows that the character is not straight, especially over money.

A large cross on the Line of the Sun, under the finger of Apollo on a pointed hand, indicates great disappointment in connection with an artistic career ; if with the other types it relates to money. On the Mount of Saturn it signifies a fatalistic and unfortunate career.

A small, well-formed cross on Jupiter's Mount, an ideal and happy marriage. The cross on the Mount of Mars under Mercury, danger of injury, caused by the enmity of another. On Mars inside the Life Line it brings accidents and personal dangers.

When on an Influence Line on Venus it announces the unhappy ending of that friendship, sometimes by an accident causing death.

A large, well-formed " Maltese Cross " between the Heart and Head Lines, called in Cheiromancy the " Mystic Cross," will give interest in mystical and poetical subjects.

Crosses on the Mount of Luna will indicate dangers in travelling by sea—when imminent there will be a break on the Fate Line. When on branch lines of the Heart it shows disappointments to the affections.

On the Head Line, danger of accident to the head ; if on a branch line, low down on the Mount of Luna, it gives an untruthful mind and sometimes self-deception.

Crosses between the Fate and Life Lines indicate changes of residence ; if nearer the Life Line than the Fate Line, the changes will be made by relatives or friends that affect one's fate ; but should these crosses be nearer the Fate Line it will show an unexpected change of environment. If the Fate and Sun Lines improve at this time, it announces a change for the better, often of house or residence. Many of these crosses will show no settled home life, while they affect the Line of Destiny.

Branches rising from all the principal lines of the hands and mounting towards the fingers indicate exuberance and riches ; they are often seen at the beginning or end of the lines. But when these branch lines are falling they indicate passing from affluence to poverty and distress. Broken or bent lines are opposing accidents, sometimes bringing sudden and unexpected death. Chains upon the lines will always indicate the weakness of that line, bringing struggles and obstacles. When on the joint of the thumb that divides the root from the second phalanx, they signify an argumentative nature.

(11) A Circle

A Circle found on the Mount of the Sun indicates a great success, leading to fame and glory. But on the lines of the hand a circle is unfavourable. On the Life or Head Line— danger to the sight or loss of an eye.

(12) The Smaller Triangle

The smaller Triangle announces aptitude for science, being a very helpful sign. When on the Mount of Jupiter it will give talent for diplomacy. On Saturn, foreknowledge—an interest in occultism.

When on the Mount of the Sun, skill in the scientific arts, medicine or architecture. On the Mount of Mercury, with a long thumb and clear Head Line, skill in arguments, making a clever barrister or politician.

When on the Mount of Mars, great talent in military tactics and engineering. On the Mount of the Moon it predicts wisdom and reason, with great intuition. When this favourable sign is seen on the Mount of Venus or the Heart Line it announces tact and cleverness in the management of the love affairs.

(13) THE GRILLE

A Grille usually announces the defects of any mount, line, or part of the hand where found. On Jupiter it gives a tendency to pride and an " uppish manner." When on Saturn, misfortune, superstition. On the Sun it announces vanity and false glory. On Mercury it indicates fraud and deception. When on the Moon it gives a wrong imagination, fancy, and foolishness.

The ancients considered this sign an obstacle to the higher principles, bringing out the materialistic or egotistical side of the nature, and was always considered an evil sign.

(14) THE LARGER TRIANGLE

The Triangle is formed by the union of the Head Line under Jupiter with the Life Line and, in the outer part near the percussion of the hand, the Line of Health.

This gives its two angles—the right and left. In some hands it is so imperfectly formed that it can be hardly seen—this is when the Line of Head is not joined to the Life Line—but instead there is a wide space between them, and sometimes there is an absence of the Health Line.

There are three angles formed on this triangle. The first or supreme angle is noticed under the first finger—it is formed by the Head Line and Life Line. When well made, clear cut and sharply defined, it gives an acute, penetrating mind and a good intellect, with a fine, noble nature. If it is an obtuse or wide angle it shows a want of intelligence, stupidity. When the angle is formed under the second finger by the Life and Head Lines, being joined together almost to the Plain of Mars, it then announces a miserable life—avaricious, apprehensive, and distrustful.

The second angle is often formed by the Life Line in conjunction with the Line of Health. It is a sign of a strong constitution if these two lines do *not* join—then the angle is formed by the Fate Line, indicating good health and success.

The third angle is formed just below the Mount of Mars, towards the top of the Mount of Luna. When clearly traced, not too red in colour, it promises a long healthy life and an intellect that can assimilate much knowledge. If the angle is very sharp it gives a tendency for nervous headaches. If very obtuse, a dull and unimaginative mind.

THE HAND

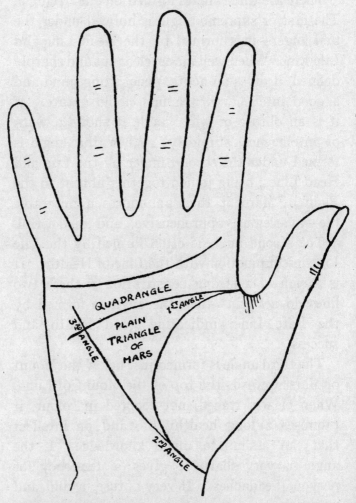

The Larger Triangle, enclosing the Plain of Mars.
The Quadrangle is the space in the palm of the hand between the Line of Head and the Line of Heart.

(15) THE QUADRANGLE

The Quadrangle is formed by the Line of the Head and the Line of the Heart. A fairly wide space between these two lines, and very broad at the side of the hand under the Mount of Mercury, indicates one who has a broad, tolerant outlook about life. If narrow in the middle it would show many prejudices, deceit, and a narrow point of view. When furrowed by many lines it signifies a nervous temperament.

If the quadrangle is absent in the hand it is a sign of misfortune.

A large cross in the quadrangle under the finger of Saturn is an inclination to mysticism. Crosses near the Fate Line in this quadrangle announce changes, and if on the outside of the hand, near the percussion, towards the Mount of the Moon, it signifies much travelling.

SECTION 10

CONCERNING THE PLANETARY
INFLUENCES ON THE HANDS

THE HAND

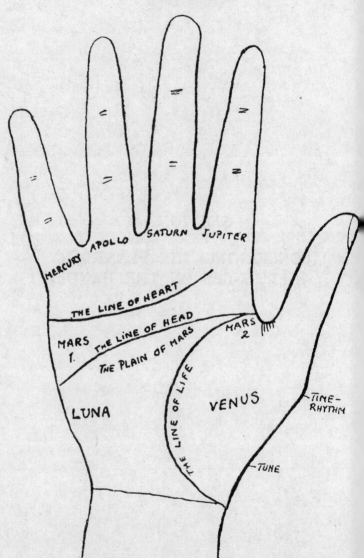

Concerning the influence of the Planets on the Mounts of the Hand.

10

CONCERNING THE PLANETARY INFLUENCES ON THE HAND

WHEN a hand is so indefinite in shape that it is difficult to make a decision as to type, often the planetary influences as indicated by a dominating mount or the length and size of one of the fingers will argue a tendency of the special influence of a planet in either its benign or malign power. The bad side of a benefic planet is like the disfavour of a good man, and the fortunate side of a malefic planet is like the approval of a bad-tempered, sulky one.

Nature's aristocracy is indicated by the benefic planets in their benign influences ; the Sun rules the third finger, dedicated to Apollo ; he announces the patrician, endowing one with beauty and grandeur of soul. The malign powers of the malefic planets by the evil aspects with the Moon indicate nature's lower class.

These intangible forces of the planets influence

the thoughts and emotions, and so form the temperament and character, and draw one into those vibrations that will make the fate, bringing the experiences that are necessary for our evolution.

> "There's a divinity that shapes our ends,
> Rough-hew them how we will."
>
> SHAKESPEARE.

(1) JUPITER

The first finger and its mount was dedicated to Jupiter by the ancient cheirosophists.

This mount or finger when noticeably prominent on a large flexible hand, with the fingers the same length as the palm, full at their base and inclined to be square tipped, with a long will phalanx to the thumb which is strong in appearance, indicates a desire to rule ; for Jupiterians are fond of power, inclining to the conventionalities, with respect for order and constitutional law.

The influence of Jupiter on this type of hand shows good judgment, practicality, one swayed by the world's opinion, appreciating material advantages, with love of home and family. The voice of the Jupiterians is gay, laughing and cheerful, at times serious, but always self-confident, giving a sociable agreeable nature, preferring to live in cities, as solitude does not attract them.

When in excess the effect will be to pervert its good characteristics, making the nature self-indulgent without caring how they attain their selfish ambitions ; and with an undeveloped mentality, then announcing conceit, vulgarity, without spirituality or honour.

The influence of only one planet on a hand is rarely seen ; more frequently there are indicated two or three strong astral powers.

Jupiter allied with Venus is the love union, indicating a happy marriage, also announcing talent for music and colour. In combination with the Moon it denotes love of literature. Mars in conjunction will give skill in military tactics or where great responsibility is indicated. Jupiter with Mercury, a gift for politics or the law, bringing honours ; Saturn also in alliance will give diplomacy and interest in religions.

When in union with Apollo, bestowing refinement of taste in dress and the environment ; and should there be a clear-cut Head Line, a brilliant mind is indicated, with noble ideas and ambitions.

Jupiter's influence makes one reliable, public-minded, not shirking responsibilities. In illness there is a tendency to inflammation of the lungs, pleurisy, gout, and apoplexy—for Jupiter rules over the head and lungs.

Jupiterians have a love of nature and are fond of animals, but are liable to accidents in regard to horses.

(2) SATURN

The second finger and mount at its base are dedicated to Saturn. Saturn indicates the Fate. This finger or mount being prominent with long fingers and knotty joints, the tips inclining to be square, gives much sense of order and talent for calculation, love of history and all things old, inclining one to form habits and live in a groove with no liking for crowds or the social life, not appreciating fine garments, being indifferent to fashion.

When the fingers are the smooth spatulate type, then there is love of mysticism. Saturn gives a solemn, slow voice, speaking with deliberation. Constant in love and faithful friends, but making unforgiving and unrelenting foes.

The illnesses Saturnians are liable to suffer from are rheumatism, biliousness, and deafness, losing the teeth in early years after much suffering. There is danger from heights and accidents through falls.

PLANETARY INFLUENCES

This melancholy planet inclines to suicide on a hand that shows a nature given to brooding and discontent. When allied with the Mount of Venus, and these two influences dominating the hand, it will then indicate love of home and country, with very little desire for change or variety, making one a loving and devoted parent, self-sacrificing and faithful. Saturn in union with Mercury will give sound judgment, with caution and discrimination. In combination with the Mount of Luna and a long sloping Head Line it inclines the nature to be mystical, romantic, looking at life from a tragic aspect, inclining sometimes to a morbid imagination, apprehensive and melancholy; when Mars is also in union, then the nature is jealous, suspicious, and quarrelsome; for the union of these three planets—Saturn, Mars, and the Moon—gives one of the most intolerant temperaments: discontented, distrustful, and intolerant; and should these three entirely dominate without the beneficent influence of Apollo, Jupiter, or Venus, or a strong, clear-cut, slightly sloping Head Line, one may expect to find a nature that is cunning, cruel, delighting in making others unhappy and depressed; obstinate in arguments, which they delight to provoke; making a dangerous, revengeful enemy. Saturn rarely gives social success, making the nature shy and self-conscious with so little *savoir-faire* in bearing and manner, the temperament being more often awkward and distrustful. As children, they should be brought into the limelight of the world and so trained to throw off these unattractive and unsuccessful traits of character.

This is the pessimistic temperament, full of fears of sadness, apprehensive of a gloomy fate. Saturn's benign influence gives wisdom and prudence, and in combination with a good Head Line can bring much success ; the malign powers of this planet bring extreme misfortune, which would be written on the Line of Fate, showing its favourable or unfavourable influence, as the signs are more or less fortunate.

(3) APOLLO—THE SUN

The third finger with the mount at its base is under the rule of the Sun.

When this is the most prominent finger or mount, with slightly pointed tips to the fingers, it indicates refinement, good judgment, and correct taste, being highly intelligent with quick perceptions, giving a tranquil, melodious voice and attractive manners, with a well-balanced nature and even temper.

In union with the Mount of Luna, inclining

to inconstancy in love and friendship, giving moods of indolence, with a liking for romantic literature ; with an indistinct Head Line, incontinuity and caprice.

When allied with Mars, greatly attracted to sport, with a tendency to be reckless and extravagant, not only with money but life itself ; for here are the gamblers—this combination giving a temper quick and passionate, but not very lasting. Apollo in union with Venus indicates one of the most fascinating, attractive natures, giving a temperament tolerant, courteous, generous, free, and understanding, with great appreciation and often talent for art and music.

Apollo—the solar god of the Ancient Greeks, the inspirer of poetry, art, and science, scattering abroad on his flood of golden flames peace among all nations—gives beauty that charms the heart, and a grace of manner, with a serenity of soul which causes love, the nature being noble and beautiful.

When allied with the " swift-winged messenger of the gods "—Mercury—then he confers love of culture, learning, and literature, giving the genius that makes for an immortal name, encouraging faith in one's " star," like all the great men of the past, giving clear and expressive ideas in speaking and writing, and easily acquiring foreign languages, a nature endowed with gifts that shine with the glorious light of intelligence and wisdom.

This is the optimistic temperament, hopeful and happy under most circumstances, being like a mirror of the sun—reflecting his radiance.

If absent, denoting a material existence, a monotonous life, like a cheerless winter's day without the sun.

The illnesses indicated by Apollo are heart and spinal complaints, for he rules the eyes and arms; bringing accidents to the limbs, but as a rule conferring a healthy and disease-resisting constitution.

(4) MERCURY

This is the fourth, the little finger, with the mount immediately beneath it.

When this Mount of Mercury is high or the finger long and straight, it will indicate a quick and alert mind, with versatility and tact, giving a joyous, lively, but feeble voice, being talkative with a rapid utterance, sometimes inclined to stammer or have difficulty in pronouncing certain words or letters.

When allied with Venus, retaining a youthful appearance all through life, being temperamentally young and buoyant, loving music and the drama; and in union with Mars, a witty and amusing personality.

Mercury and the Sun allied denotes the writer, artist, or musician, giving enchanting powers of eloquence and vivacity.

The combination of Mercury and the Moon indicates imagination and romance, a restless nature, desiring changes, preferring travel to the home life, not being domesticated.

Mercurians have a great aptitude for science and are clever at business, being industrious, intelligent, with quick, penetrating minds and the capacity for making use of opportunties and people. When Mercury is very long in proportion to the other fingers or the mount extremely high, in combination with Saturn and Mars, it inclines the nature to be unscrupulous and pretentious, using people and circumstances for the advantages to be gained, with a temper excitable and uncontrolled, crafty and malicious.

The absence of this mount and an insignificant little finger shows a useless life, with little determination or perseverance, inaptitude for science or commerce.

The illnesses Mercurians have a tendency to are brain diseases, insanity, impediment of speech, and maladies of the liver and kidneys. Also accidents through sport and games, Mercury ruling over the legs.

(5) Venus

The Mount of Venus, which is formed by the root of the thumb, signifies, when fairly developed, a desire to please and of being loved, tenderness, delighting in beautiful forms, colour, and love of melody in music. In union with Mars it inspires passion but does not give fidelity, making for inconstancy with a desire for material pleasures, sensuality, vanity, and coquetry. When in combination with the Mount of Luna it denotes idleness ; either mount being in excess, debauchery.

Venus gives a soft, tender, rather drawling, sweet voice, with a feminine type of beauty, the hands being smooth, with pointed fingers and dimpled joints, the third phalanges full and shell-pink filbert nails. The musical composers, artists, orators, writers, and poets are inspired by Venus with the gift of pathos and emotion, " holding the mirror up to nature," and so reflecting her moods of love, tenderness, and devotion, bringing the tears to one's eyes, drawing intense sympathy and admiration by their depth of feeling, passion, and genius.

PLANETARY INFLUENCES

Venus in union with Apollo gives appreciation of culture and learning, also love of pleasure ; being very attractive and demonstrative, taking delight in beautiful clothes, scents, and flowers.

Venus in conjunction with the Mount of Saturn, or that finger long and inclined to be square, will add depth and seriousness, making the nature more thoughtful, prudent, and constant. When with Mercury, either the finger well developed or the mount broad or high, it indicates social adaptability, the mind influenced by beauty of form and colour, and endowing the temperament with charm and grace, giving a youthful and buoyant personality, being attracted to youth and in sympathy with those younger. Saturn makes one more fond of those older—for the planet that Venus aspects indicates the type that attracts and fascinates in the love affairs, this being shown in the hand by the mounts or length of one particular fi ger.

In absence it indicates a cold, unsympathetic nature, without tenderness or devotion.

The illnesses denoted by Venus are hysteria, depressed emotional conditions, and feminine disorders. When this mount is small or very flat it indicates a poor constitution and want of vitality.

(6) Mars

Cheiromancy gives two mounts on the hand to Mars, representing active and passive courage in the character.

The Mount of Mars that indicates moral courage is at the side of the hand opposite the thumb, just below the Mount of Mercury, and when fairly developed it endows the temperament with patience, endurance, self-sacrifice, and devotion ; in excess it gives the martyr-like natures. The absence of this mount de-denotes impatience, want of resignation and self-command, with little strength of resistance against evil.

The other Mount of Mars is found in the hand, inside the Life Line, immediately under the Mount of Jupiter. It gives physical courage, coolness in danger, resolution, impetuosity ; in excess, cruelty, anger, and tyranny ; in absence, cowardice, want of self-control.

When Mars is the ruling influence of the temperament it confers energy and unconventionality, giving a loud, blustering voice, and making one, when angry, rude, harsh, and wrathful. These hands are hard, with dry red skins, the fingers thick, with the Mounts of Mars high and rayed with lines and crosses. When very prominent, one is inclined to be too forceful, aggressive, with love of domineering, enjoying all contests. The temperament is matter of fact, with little imagination or sympathy, and a great dislike to any kind of restraint, the nature being undisciplined. In excess it indicates a headstrong, restless, and unsettled character, leading a wandering life, preferring noise and tumult with an element of danger, rarely caring for domesticity ; and with the line of dissipation deeply marked, an inherited tendency for stimulants.

With short square nails and the thumb thick it denotes a quarrelsome and revengeful nature. As a rule Mars confers robust health—illness more often occurring through accidents, then making one liable to acute and sharp attacks of pain, with a feverish tendency. It also gives a passion for sport, and occupation connected with horses and dogs.

When Mars is in combination with the Mount of Mercury it indicates a liking for engineering and motoring or work that requires much physical energy, giving love of movement. When in union with the Mount of Luna it indicates much travelling.

Mars in combination with Mercury and Jupiter makes the nature very self-reliant, being well able to fight one's own battles and take care of one's self. The love brought by Mars and Venus is more passionate, fierce, and jealous than romantic, tender, or loving ; it also confers love of music, dramatic power, and a liking for vivid colour. Mars in union with any of the other planets will impart movement, energy, and activity to that particular planet represented in the hand by the mounts.

Mars-Apollo and Mercury make the clever surgeons and doctors.

Mars-Jupiter and Mercury or the Moon, the powerful and impressive orators and preachers.

Mars-Saturn and the Moon will give a great liking for agriculture or colonial life.

Mars-Venus and the Moon will confer histrionic talent on a clever hand, inspiring one with dramatic powers.

Mars and Saturn are the destructive forces in nature ; Apollo, Venus, and Jupiter constructive. These combinations and varieties that exist in nature account for the differences of temperament to be found in the race of man. The malefic planets are not in harmony with mankind, being of use to the same moderate extent as the skilful physician who uses poisons in order to effect cures.

PLANETARY INFLUENCES

(7) THE MOON

The Mount of Luna is found immediately below that of Mars, on the percussion of the hand. When fairly well developed it gives sympathy, imagination, with love of mysticism, often having prophetic dreams; in excess, quick fanciful conceptions, but with little logic in the ideas, day-dreaming and indolent. The absence of this mount indicates want of poetry and sympathy, having little imagination, cold, capricious, egotistical temperaments and not very practical, having a restless, dissatisfied nature and a longing for new pleasures—merely from idle curiosity or caprice, not through passion or desire, denoting vanity and conceit.

The Moon in union with Mars denotes bad temper, insolent in manner, untruthful and faithless. Saturn in combination indicates a temper that shows in senseless talk and evil speaking, having a morbid desire to injure another by evil insinuation—making for cowardice in danger. The hands are soft, white, and plump, with the Mount of Luna dominating the palm of the hand. When in union with Jupiter it indicates a gentle, sympathetic, emotional nature, fond of literature. In love and friendship being inconstant, and swayed by moods.

The Mount of Luna dominating on a pointed hand with a supple thumb gives a love of collecting curios and old china ; and when in union with Venus, inspiring a talent for art and music of a fantastic nature.

The Moon gives a low, plaintive, and indifferent tone to the voice.

This Mount of Luna prominent indicates liability to accidents by water, and illnesses of the nature of consumption and lunacy, and weakness of the stomach and intestines. With Saturn, paralysis and epilepsy.

THE ART OF INTERPRETATION

THE ART OF INTERPRETATION

" In arming yourself with this science, you arm yourself with a great power and you will have a thread that will guide you into the labyrinth of the most impenetrable hearts."—HENRI DE BALZAC.

CHEIROMANCY is the looking-glass in which one sees reflected the true self without the illusions of the outer self or personality.

For to " know thyself " one must find this reflection away from the complacent and indulgent ideas of self, and it is not always a reliable impression that is given by the adoration of love and the praises of admiring friends, or the criticism and detraction of enemies.

There is great help to be gained by the study of these old occult sciences, for they are true counsellors and unflattering ; and in finding out the faults they also point out the way in which these may be remedied—progress being the most essential part of the life.

THE HAND

In forming an opinion and making a general judgment of a hand one should first consider the formation and type. Then look at the thumb, for this part of the hand is first in importance in Cheiromancy, representing the great motive powers of the life—which are the Will, Judgment, Love, and Sympathy. Examine the fingers next and notice which of the three worlds predominate—Soul, Mind, or the Material—then look at the extremity of the fingers, whether elementary, spatulate, square, pointed, or mixed, and their formation, either smooth or knotty, showing impulse and inspiration, or reflection, order, and a philosophical inclination. Regard their length in relation to the palm—see whether the palm has greater length than the fingers, or if the fingers and the palm are well proportioned ; then look to the constituency of the hand, whether soft or hard—indicating an indolent or active temperament. After this examine the mounts, seeing how they encroach or lean towards one another and which is most in evidence, showing the ruling passion of the life—it may be for art, science, music, or business ; imagination, love, romance, power, wealth, and ambition.

To understand if the desires are likely to be realised one must interrogate the lines and symbols of the hands. These signs reveal the probabilities of the success or failure of the wishes. Concentrate on the course of the seven principal lines. The Head Line is important, as it indicates the trend of the character and the development of the mentality towards the practical side ; for when this line is seen passing over the Mount of Mars on the percussion of the hand, it bestows much mental energy and a desire for the realities of the material side of life. If turning down to the Mount of Luna, then it indicates the love of the ideal ; a weak Head Line with this formation denotes little desire to cultivate the talents, undeveloped mental energy—on a soft hand indolence and idleness ; if also wide apart from the Life Line at the beginning it announces a thoughtless, heedless outlook on life, one's own enemy—the foolish virgin.

It is not a good sign for the Head Line to be too straight, for then it indicates selfishness, greed and avarice, often giving an unsympathetic, hard, and cruel mind, especially with a big thumb ; living entirely for personal gain. The reverse to this is denoted by the long sloping Head Line, letting opportunities pass by through want of mental energy ; and when starting with a wide space from the Life Line it indicates a want of thought about the affairs of life, making for stupidity and vanity.

The Life and Health Line should be consulted when considering the length of life, with freedom from illnesses, for they show the vitality and natural powers to resist disease. The Heart Line and Influence Lines will indicate the happiness or disappointments of the love affairs.

For the success of the fortune follow the Line of Fate or Saturnian Line in its course, noting the place where it is joined, deeply or faintly, by other lines, and their power of breaking, arresting, or cutting through this line and so opposing and interfering with its success, indicating great obstacles to the realisation of the wishes and desires in either health, love, money, or ambition. This Line of Fate deeply engraven on the hand, rising up to the mounts and passing through all these opposing signs, indicates that it is strongly protected. If ending on the Mount of Saturn, then it announces an unassailable and an assured position. When broken, arrested, or winding and uncertain in its course, the other lines will reveal the cause of these impediments to success ; where the Line of Fate recovers from these irregularities will mark the epoch in the life when the fortune will straighten out and improve.

The next line to be observed is the Line of Apollo or the Sun. When beginning from the Magic Bracelet or the Mount of Luna it sometimes corrects and compensates for the ill-luck of a weak Fate Line ; but it does not promise such a secure, safe, or reliable fortune as a powerful Fate Line, though it can confer much fame, glory, and celebrity.

With a clever and well-developed hand, strong branch lines rising from the Life Line or Head Line, sweeping through the hand up to the mounts, often replacing an unfortunate Saturnian Line, show the talents are well employed, being endowed with the energy to work out new enterprises after passing through disappointments and false hopes borne with calmness and resignation, and rising upon the wings of faith and courage to other ideas, bringing success and happiness.

All these lines and signs in a hand are to be understood as running concurrently, the one with the other.

After examining the lesser lines and the symbols—which are the Stars, Squares, Crosses, Circles, Points, Islands, Chains, Grilles, and Triangles—modify them according to their position on the hand. Then consider the hand in its entirety, returning to the generality of the mounts, lines, and signs—bearing in mind that the mounts well placed, not too prominent, are one of the signs of good fortune.

A single line clearly and finely traced, of a vivid colour, indicates success to that line.

Two lines crossed indicates misfortune. Three lines at an equal distance, rising to the fingers, of equal power and uncrossed, announce fame, success, and great good fortune. Should these same lines be unequal, broken and tortuous, crossed or barred, then are indicated struggles, misfortunes, and much unhappiness. Straight, clear and finely-cut lines, rising up towards the mounts, are always a favourable sign.

A multitude of lines signify an intense but highly-strung temperament—living with a strain on the nervous system.

When a long, straight line—well-coloured and looking a little luminous—starts from the Mount of Venus and goes directly to the Mount of Mercury, clear, without obstacles, it is one of the happiest signs in a hand, being the union of Mercury and Venus — love, fortune, and happiness.

Paracelsus says : " When the lines are luminous, or these vivid lights are seen in a hand, they indicate much good." Attach importance to the colour of the lines, for when they are light red they denote good health and a long life—giving an active temperament. Pale lines indicate indolence ; when very pale and dry in appearance, a poor condition of the blood.

Livid, dark or blue lines are the sign of a melancholy disposition and often bad health, with blood disorders and liver troubles.

The right hand should confirm what the left hand indicates. Should the *right* be clearer and more distinct in its markings than the left, then the fate will be more fortunate than is anticipated ; but should the *left* be stronger and more distinct than the right in its tracings and scores, then it denotes that the destiny will not work out according to the wishes and desires.

Details of events are marked to a greater degree on the left hand as a rule, the right hand indicating the general success of the life, and trend of events. It is a more hopeful and assured sign for the realisation of the ambitions —whether in health, love, or money—if *both* hands agree.

When there is great talent denoted on the left hand—and this is principally seen by a remarkable Head Line—but very faintly traced on the right, then it shows that the inherited talents and gifts have not been cultivated ; but where the right hand shows the starting of clearer, brighter lines, it will indicate the epoch in the life when one begins to develop the talents.

At whatever age the Line of the Sun comes into the hand, the life will then hold greater interests, making the pathway more brilliant and successful—like a day of summer's sunshine compared with a dull and dreary winter's day. It also shows that the character is developing, denoting a more reliable personality.

Finely-traced and deeply-cut lines indicate fine ideas and perceptions with a deep and culti-vated intellect, giving refinement of thought and manner ; broad, coarse lines denote the opposite, giving greater physical activity.

One of the most important characteristics of the hand is its *flexibility*, for this indicates a mind with elasticity, perspicuity, and perspicacity ; but a hand beautiful in formation, colour, and shape, if stiff and set, inflexible and unsupple, with the fingers clinging close together and the thumb set high and turned inwards, denotes a mind and personality that does not expand— one who lives in a groove of traditions, obstinate, often stupid, boring, and tiresome to live with.

A hand beautiful in proportion and shape, *flexible* and pliant, but not too supple, will indicate a clever, interesting personality with refinement, good taste, wit, clear intuition, alert, and understanding.

Aristotle said : " The lines are not written without cause in the hand of man, but come from celestial influences and the peculiar human individuality."

The ancient writers on Cheiromancy—notably the Brahmins of India—connected these lines in the hands with the astral powers, and held that they influence the sub-conscious mind of man and the universal soul of nature, pervading all substances—not only the physical but the intellectual and emotional worlds of our being.

" To understand this old occult science it must be continually practised, merely reading books on the subject will not be sufficient," says one of the old writers on palmistry. " Personal experiment," said Coleridge, " is necessary in order to correct our own observations of the experiments which nature herself makes for us."

D'Arpentigny said : " The real nature of man will lay buried a great time, discovering itself unawares and of necessity, proving the principles of this science of Cheirosophy."

One must also be prepared to learn the good and the evil, which is hidden in these lines and symbols, for without the contrast of evil we should not appreciate the good.

THE HAND

Before making a definite decision one should take a *résumé* of the whole of the hand. The work finished, then say fearlessly, kindly, what you honestly, sub-consciously feel is the truth of your deductions and calculations.

Ptolemy says : " Judgment must be regulated by thyself as well as by the science."

" Love and hatred prohibit the true accomplishment of judgment, and, inasmuch as they lessen the most important, so likewise do they magnify the most trivial things."

ΕΚ ΤΕΛΕΟΣ ΑΡΧΗ

PLATE VIII

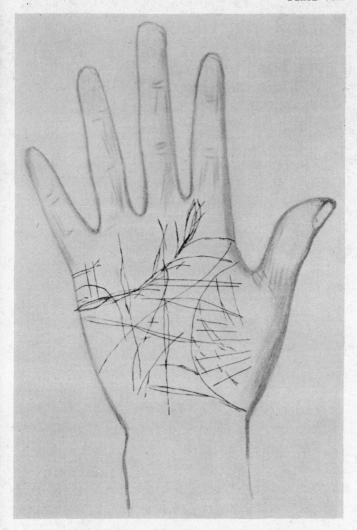

THE UNLUCKY SIGNS AND SYMBOLS IN LOVE AND FRIENDSHIP

The Influence Lines on Venus forked and turning away from the Life Line. Note the Island at the beginning and ending of the Heart Line, also the Influence Lines to the Fate Line, which, being barred and cut through, denote unfortunate attachments. The Marriage Lines on Mercury are unfortunate signs.

PLATE IX

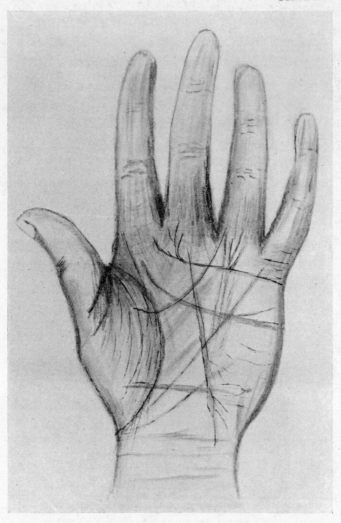

The hand of a musical comedy actress, born of humble parents. She married the heir of an old and noble family.

PLATE X

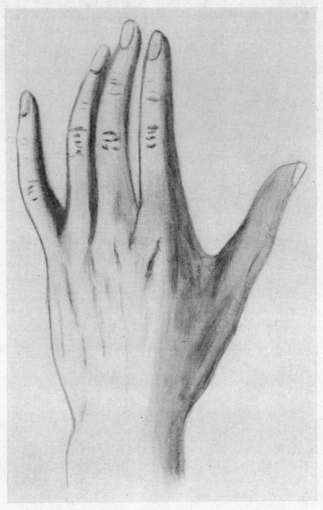

A woman's hand: a type more often seen among the old families of the nobility.

PLATE XI

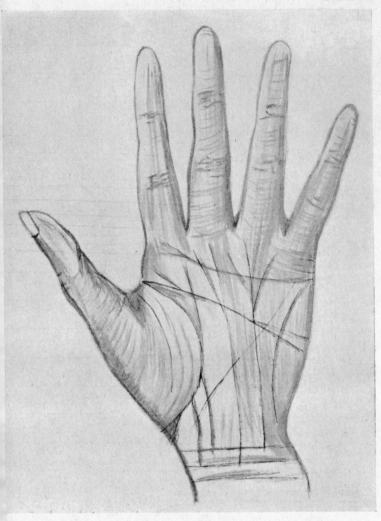

The principal lines to be seen on the hand of an actress who was world-famous for her great histrionic talents.

PLATE XII

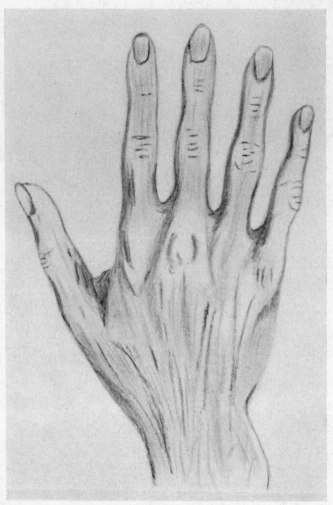

The hand of one who preferred the spiritual to the material life. By descent "the daughter of a hundred Earls" and of one of the most powerful noble families in England.

PLATE XIII

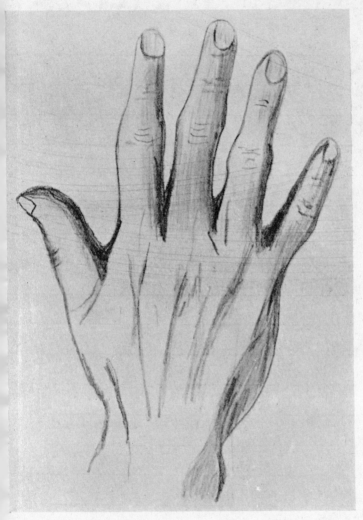

The hand of a maid, who was punctual, orderly (shown by the developed joints), with good manners (conical tips to the fingers), always neatly dressed and the hair tidy! Energetic nd obliging (broad palm).

PLATE XIV

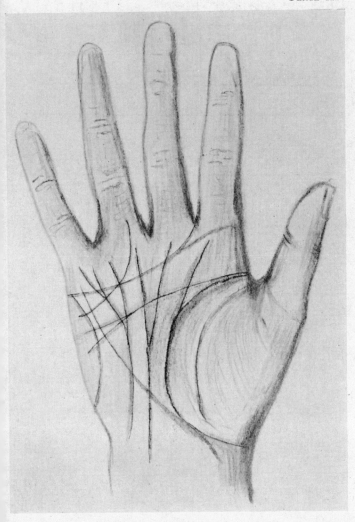

The hand of a famous writer who wrote, when quite young, a novel that eventually became a world classic. The line indicating this great talent is the clear forked Line of the Head, one branch falling to the Mount of Luna—indicating the inherent imaginative and creative artistic faculties—and the other branch passing over the Mount of Mars—denoting great mental energy. This shaped hand denotes a romantic, artistic temperament, with spontaneity of thought. The nail phalanx of the little finger, long and pointed, with this type of thumb and Line of the Head, endow one with untiring energy in seeking for perfection, in the way of expressing the thoughts and ideas. The curving line from Mars to Apollo is often to be seen on the hands of those that create their own success and fortunes, giving, on this shaped hand, the power to use the artistic talents in a practical direction. This type of Head Line indicates mental application and concentration, with continuity of thought and tenacity of purpose.

PLATE XV

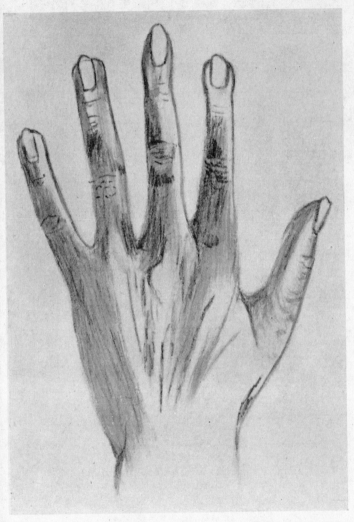

THE HAND OF A FAMOUS RUSSIAN DANCER

PLATE XVI

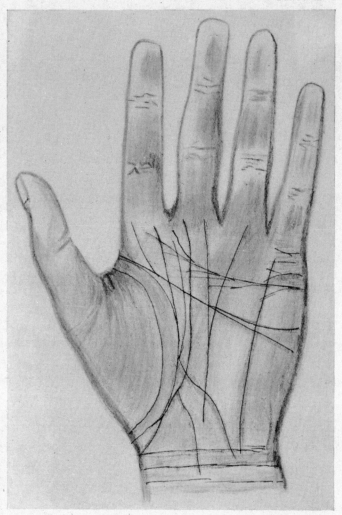

The hand of one of England's most illustrious officers, who has survived all attacks made by either the sword or the pen ! The lines rising from the Life Line—with this shaped thumb and Head Line—indicate inherent talents, foreshadowing great success in the career.

PLATE XVII

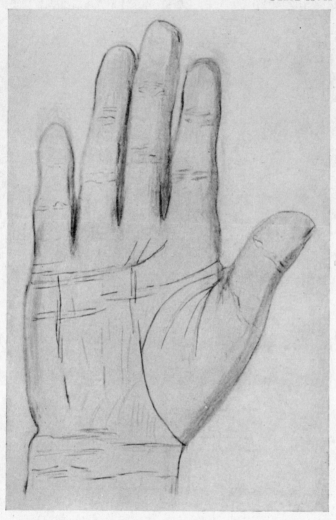

The hand of a gardener. The few lines on the palm, and the short thumb, are characteristic of the labouring classes.

PLATE XVIII

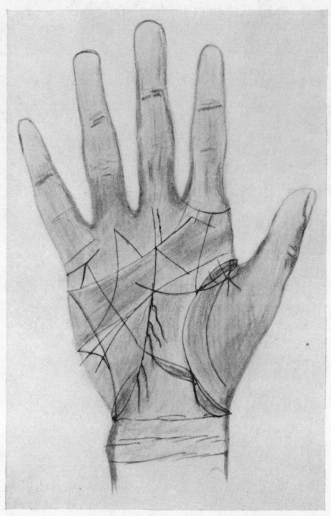

This is the hand of one who is endowed with the faculty of prescience, indicated by so many lines forming triangles with the points turned upwards—denoting spiritual concentration. The unfortunate Line of Fate, and also the Line of Life, starting with islands, show the loss of parents and fortune in the early years. Both grandfathers left large fortunes, but through the wrong judgment of lawyers and the carelessness of trustees most of it was lost. This is indicated by the falling lines from the Line of Fate, which denote loss of money by treachery. It was only a firm reliance on the Divine powers that prevented the disasters written on this unfortunate Line of Fate. The mystery about this hand is that as the fortunes improved, so many of the islands gradually turned into triangles.

The long nail phalanges to the fingers denote the channel to the spirit world, conferring psychic powers. The Square on Jupiter, with Solomon's Ring, also the triangle at the end of the Head Line, give wisdom. The Fate, Head, and Hepatic lines forming a triangle endow one with intuition.

PLATE XIX

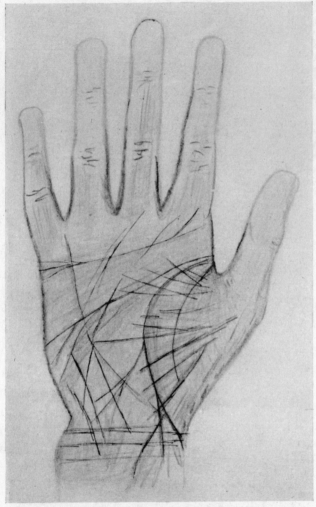

This is the hand of one who came of an old soldier family, and the fourth generation of his race to die on the battle-field for England. Temperamently fond of a comfortable life, especially warmth; and yet all through two winters he stood for hours in the slough of the trenches, overcoming the temperament by character. This is indicated by the strong thumb and powerful Head Line. The rays from Mars crossing the Life Line and breaking the Fate Line portend a violent death. Note the long idealistic Heart Line (unfolded in this life as an adoring love for his mother, who lay dying of cancer at the time of the Great War and so adding to his sorrow and anxiety—this being denoted by the falling lines at the end of the Head Line, and the deep scores on the Mount of Venus).

PLATE XX

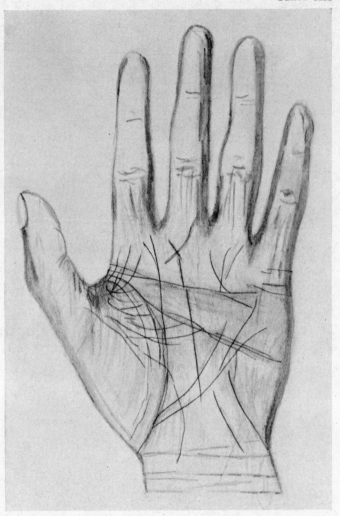

The hand of an officer in the Guards, twice wounded and eventually killed in the Great War. The rays on the Mount of Mars under Jupiter, and the islands on the Head Line, foreshadowed the wounds and mental stress. The line rising to Jupiter from the Life Line shows responsibilities well carried out in spite of personal sufferings. It is the strongest line in the hand.

PLATE XXI

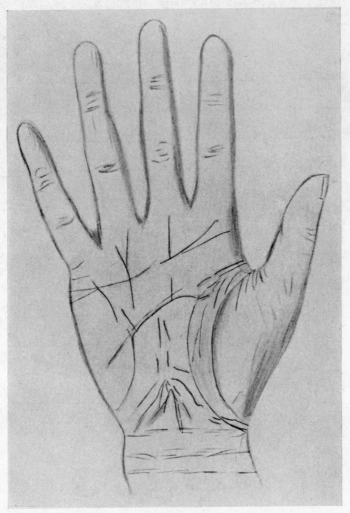

The hand of a young man, heir to a dukedom, killed in the Great War. The breaks on the Head and Fate Lines foreshadowed early death by accident or violence. Otherwise, with such a good Line of Life he would have lived to old age.

PLATE XXII

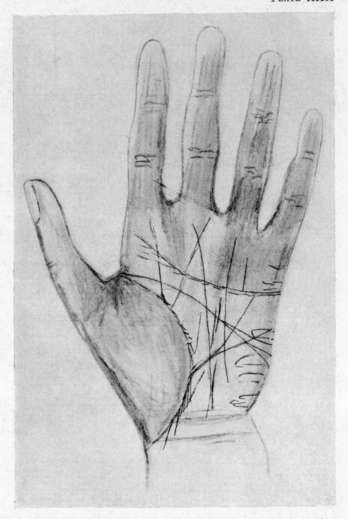

The hand of an Italian prince who died of consumption brought on by the hardships of war. The feathered Heart and Life Lines show a delicate constitution : the Health Line deeply cutting into the Life Line indicating that bad health was undermining his life. Note the long islands on the Mount of Luna—on hands of this shape denoting an inherited tendency to consumption.

PLATE XXIII

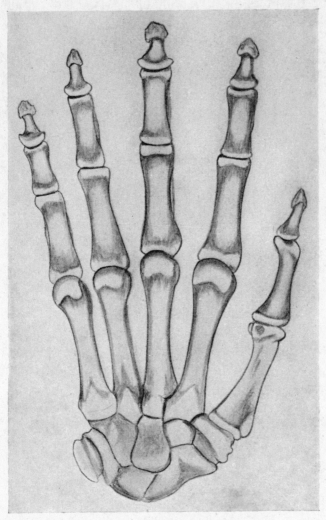

"Peace ! the song of woe is after all an earthly song."—TENNYSON.